Dear fellow Weight Watcher,

You may have heard me say that, for me, counting SmartPoints has been a game changer. But do you want to know the real truth? It's actually been a life changer. I joined Weight Watchers more than a year ago, and I'm still marveling at how it's given me a new way of thinking, of eating, of being.

I've done a lot of dieting in my time, and I didn't enjoy any of it. That's why I love Weight Watchers: It isn't about dieting. It's about making choices that make you healthier and happier. There are days when I go over my points and days when I stay under, but I'm always accountable. SmartPoints keep me ever aware of how I'm treating my body.

The results have been consistent, steady, and so rewarding. I never feel deprived. Or punished. I feel in control, revitalized, and yes, definitely happier. Weight Watchers has helped me finally master the food game. And I'm struck by how effortless it's been.

That effortlessness—the sense that I'm getting where I want to be without having to sacrifice—is what inspired this cookbook. After hearing so many friends and family members say how delicious the food at my table is—not "diet" tasting at all—I decided to gather some of my favorite chefs and share the recipes that satisfy and nurture me with their goodness.

I'm confident they'll do the same for you. I love the idea of us all eating deliciously together. And, yes, every recipe includes SmartPoints! Enjoy!

"REAL COOKING IS
AN ART FORM. A GIFT
TO BE SHARED."
—OPRAH WINFREY

FOOD
HEALTH
— AND —
HAPPINESS

115 ON-POINT RECIPES FOR GREAT MEALS AND A BETTER LIFE

OPRAH
WINFREY

— WITH LISA KOGAN —

PUBLISHED BY

FLATIRON
BOOKS
NEW YORK

AN
OPRAH
BOOK

PRODUCED BY

MELCHER
MEDIA

www.flatironbooks.com

Library of Congress Cataloging-in-Publication Data available upon request.

ISBN 9781250140173

Our books may be purchased in bulk for promotional, educational, or business use.
Please contact your local bookseller or the Macmillan Corporate and
Premium Sales Department at 1-800-221-7945, extension 5442, or by e-mail at
MacmillanSpecialMarkets@macmillan.com.

**MELCHER
MEDIA**

Produced by
Melcher Media
124 West 13th Street
New York, NY 10011
www.melcher.com

Contributing writer: Lisa Kogan
Cover and interior design: Trina Bentley of Make & Matter
Cover photography: Ruven Afanador

First Edition: January 2017

10 9 8 7 6 5 4 3 2 1

I treasure words. So the making of a book
is an act of reverence for me.

Thank you to all who helped make this book a
tangible thing to behold, especially Lisa Kogan,
wordsmith and chief humorist.

Charles Melcher, Aaron Kenedi, and the
Melcher team for your artful guidance.

Adam Glassman, Jenny Capitain,
Ruven Afanador, and Urania Greene for
our beautiful shots at dawn.

Bob Greene and all the chefs featured on
page 225. Without you there wouldn't be a book.

And a special love shout-out to Stedman
Graham, who—no matter what meal I prepare—
always says, "Honey, that's the best I ever had."

—OPRAH WINFREY

TABLE OF CONTENTS

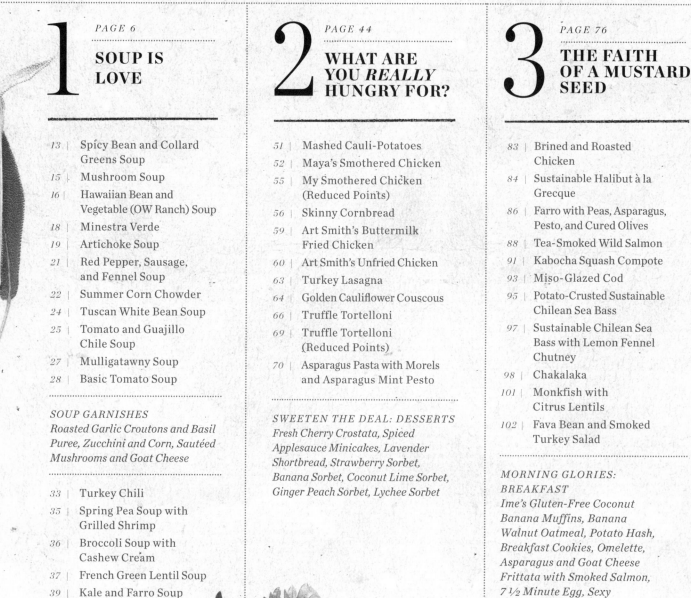

WHEN I KNOW BETTER, I DO BETTER

Maya Angelou, my wonderfully wise mother-sister-friend, once said, "When you know better, you do better." Well, I thought I knew all there was to know about losing weight. Over the years I'd interviewed every expert, I'd tried every diet. For one brief moment, back in 1988, it seemed like I'd found the secret: After a four-month liquid diet (which is a nice way of saying: fast), I practically leapt onto the stage of my show to reveal my brand-new body in a pair of skinny-minnie Calvin Klein jeans. To prove the point, I hauled out a little red wagon loaded with actual fat representing the pounds I'd starved myself to lose.

And then—no pun intended—I fell off the wagon. As of course I was bound to do, I started eating again. I lied to myself. I broke promises to myself. I beat myself up. I let myself down. I felt like a spectacular failure. And the worst part was, I did this over and over again. My lowest moment came the year I was afraid to win an Emmy; I couldn't stand to think how fat I'd look to all the pretty soap stars in the audience if I had to waddle up to the podium. It didn't matter that I'd be wearing hand-tailored couture. In my mind, to my shame, I'd be dressed in fat.

If Maya were here right now (and as I sit writing this, I like to believe she is), I'd say, "OK, if anyone knows better when it comes to dieting, it's me. So how do you explain my endless struggles with weight? Why is it that with all this experience and information, I haven't done better?" My guess is she'd probably smile and, in that commanding voice unlike any I've ever heard,

she'd say, "Well, my dear, when you're truly ready to know, you will." And as usual, she'd be absolutely right.

You can tell yourself to eat less and move more, you can cut down on carbs (so long, lasagna) and salty snacks (goodbye, Mr. Chips), you can practice portion control and begin the day with a balanced breakfast—at this point we all know the drill. But it's one thing to be able to recite the rules of dieting, and quite another to fully internalize and know the truth of maintaining a healthy weight.

The reality is that for most of us, diets are a temporary solution at best. They last as long as our willpower holds out. But how long can any of us hold our breath before we need a gulp of air? I've fallen into every trap, from "The diet starts first thing Monday morning" to "I'll have the cheeseburger and fries—with a diet soda, please." Yes, I've made every excuse in the book. The most recent: when I hurt my ankle while hiking in the

Winning the Emmy in 1992 was a professional high point. Unfortunately my weight was also at a high point.

Maya Angelou always had a home-cooked meal, an honest assessment of every situation, and a warm embrace waiting for me.

Me, my Calvins, and that infamous wagon of fat turned out to be iconic television. But if I had it to do again— I wouldn't!

My all time favorite place to be is quietly under a tree. I sit every day in praise and gratitude for all life's blessings.

wrong shoes. Afterwards, I couldn't exercise enough to burn even one calorie. But rather than just be extra vigilant and eat extra sensibly, here's what I told myself: "You really should get back to protein shakes. Skip breakfast. Skip lunch. Avoid alcohol. Enough with the carbs. Do a cleanse." Which quickly morphed into: "I'm on vacation, though! I have a house full of guests. We're serving a buffet for breakfast. And it starts with pancakes and cronuts and bacon. But it's true that I have to make better choices. I know! I'll choose the turkey bacon...and maybe just a jalapeño cheddar cheese bagel and one scoop of scrambled eggs with truffle. And some melon, because melon is super healthy, and..." Try that for a week with minimal physical exertion and I'm here to tell you, it's a half-pound-a-day weight gain, easy.

That's where I was in the summer of 2015 when Weight Watchers called. Seventeen pounds beyond my already steadily overweight weight. And yes, you read that right—Weight Watchers actually called me!

For years, my daily prayer had been, "Lord, what should I do next? I've tried everything already. Twice." So I not only took the call from Weight Watchers—I decided to take it as the answer to my prayer. The call came, and I was ready to listen. Something inside me shifted. The need to see a certain number on the scale, to wear a specific size, had somehow fallen away and released me. How exhilarating to suddenly think I might be able to stop being a slave to yo-yo dieting, that I might be able to live freely and independently, eating the way I chose in order to fuel my life! I could be free from the burden of stressing out over what to eat next, free from the guilt of regretting what I'd just eaten. Somewhere buried beneath the decades of trial and error—the seesawing between fat and fasting, feast and famine, the shame and fear and frustration—was a belief that I could find balance and satisfaction with food without having to declare war on myself. I dreamed of detente, of eating with pleasure, ease, and maybe even a hint of joy.

"AS LONG AS I CAN REMEMBER,
I'VE BEEN THE KIND OF PERSON
WHO WANTS TO SHARE THE THINGS
THAT MAKE LIFE BETTER."

— O P R A H   W I N F R E Y

I know now that losing weight and keeping it off will never be about dieting and deprivation, shaming and guilting yourself. My friend Marianne Williamson was right when she wrote me a letter saying that you have to change the way you think, not just about food, but about the whole of your life. Getting real relief from the burden of extra pounds requires what another friend, Bob Greene, tried to teach me years ago: In order to wake up to a new way of eating, moving, and being with yourself, you must first recognize that you deserve to be healthy and you're worthy of being loved. You have to be willing to give yourself the best care you can, every day.

These are ideas that demand a new consciousness.

For me, more than anything, that means really feeling what I feel. No more masking or avoiding my anxiety—or anger, or sadness, or fear of confrontation—with a bag of chips or a handful of nuts. For most of my life, emotional eating has been my negative behavioral hot button. I've only recently learned to process and not repress with food whatever I'm experiencing that's uncomfortable. All the years when my regular routine included taping at least two and sometimes three shows a day, people would ask how I managed the stress, and I'd say, "I don't feel stress." I never felt it because I ate it. Just the slightest inkling of discomfort—a phone call I didn't want to make, an encounter that might result in a less than pleasing outcome—would have me reaching for something salty or crunchy, and feeling immediately comforted and soothed. Unwanted emotion triggers unwanted behavior.

Now, I've learned to do so much better. I not only feel what I feel—when appropriate, I speak it out loud. When I have to make a hard decision, I lean right into it, rather than procrastinating and burying stuff that later shows up in my thighs. For sure, it's a new way of being.

This new consciousness extends to how I eat—and this is where Weight Watchers has been so helpful. It's a really effective tool for being more aware of the food I put on my plate and in my mouth. It's not a diet. You can eat anything you want—and I do. I use the point system like a game (for more information on the Weight Watchers point system go to page 224). I get 30 points a day to play with as I like. The healthier my choices, the more plays I get.

As long as I can remember, I've been the kind of person who wants to share the things that make life better. When I come upon something useful, something that brings me pleasure or comfort or ease, I want everyone else to know about it and benefit from it, too. And that is how this cookbook came to be. It's part of my life story—the lessons I've learned, the discoveries I've made—told through food. The most important discovery: that it's possible to come to sane and sustainable terms with eating. That you can master the food game with points, nutrition, and above all, deliciousness. Because if what you eat is just mediocre, it will always leave you wanting.

Many of the recipes that follow are from the wonderful chefs I've been blessed to know and work with over the years. I make a lot of these dishes myself, to feed my family and friends; for me, there's nothing better than having the people you love gathered around the table for a home-cooked meal. These are the dishes I've served for major celebrations and for no reason at all. I hope you'll enjoy making them, savor eating them, and delight in sharing them. Because what I now know for sure: Food is supposed to be about joy, not suffering. It's meant to nourish and sustain us, not cause us pain. When you eat consciously and well, you feed your body and your spirit. And that makes all life more delicious!

Cheers to your health, happiness, and conscious enjoyment!

CHAPTER

1

SOUP IS
LOVE

IT'S SUNDAY NIGHT AT 7:00 SHARP, AND I'M SIX YEARS OLD.

Or maybe I'm eight. I could even be nine. No matter—whatever my age, I can tell you exactly what I was doing at 7 p.m. on just about every single Sunday of my childhood. I was sitting in front of the Magnavox riveted to what was, at the time, the greatest show on earth: *Lassie*. For 30 minutes— well, 22 once you subtracted the commercials—everything else melted away; it was just me and the Martin family and the most devoted dog ever.

All I knew for sure in those days was that my world would be perfect and we'd all live happily ever after as the credits rolled if my mom would ladle up a great big bowl of Campbell's soup just for me.

Almost every day for lunch I now have soup.

Let's just say that Timmy Martin was not an easy child. That boy was constantly dangling from cliffs, getting trapped in abandoned mine shafts, falling into rivers—I think he even managed to sink into quicksand once or twice. But that was OK because whatever happened to Timmy, you knew Lassie had his back. Now, you might think that seeing the most brilliant collie on earth rescue her master from certain death in a pit of quicksand would be the high point of an episode—but not for me. My favorite part always came at the very end, when Timmy's mother would tousle his hair, give him a gentle lecture about how he should really make more of an effort to avoid falling into badger holes, and serve him a piping hot bowl of Campbell's soup, which was by all accounts *mmm mmm* good!

It was particularly *mmm mmm* good for Campbell's—which, I would later learn, sponsored *Lassie* for 19 years. But back then, in Milwaukee, product placement was the furthest thing from my mind. All I knew for sure in those days was that my world would be perfect and we'd all live happily ever after as the credits rolled if my mom would ladle up a great big bowl of Campbell's soup just for me.

My mother was a maid. After spending all day cleaning other people's houses, tousling my braids and serving me soup with a smile was out of the question. Even wishing such a thing was absurd. My mom did the best

One time, Lassie was lost for weeks. Every night I'd be on my knees praying she'd survive. Years later, it dawned on me that the cliffhangers always coincided with the TV sweeps period!

I was glued to our old Magnavox during Lassie, but I refused to even blink if The Supremes or The Jackson Five were on Ed Sullivan.

Here I am on my Aunt Susie Mae's front porch in Kosciusko, Mississippi. I spent a lot of time on that porch, and I still think of her whenever I'm in the rocking chair on my own porch.

This is one of only a handful of shots from my childhood. I think I was around three or four, and I was so happy to be wearing patent leather shoes.

she could do, but to this day I have clear memories of putting grape Kool-Aid on my cereal because we were too broke to buy milk. The truth is, I remember times when we couldn't afford any food.

I wanted a different life. I wanted to feel safe. I wanted to feel understood. I wanted a world of possibility and unconditional love. Do you see what I'm getting at? I wanted soup.

As children, we don't get to pick the ways in which we're loved. But then we grow up, and if we're smart and prepared and very determined, every once in a while we actually do get the life we wanted. In my case, that life has included more possibilities than I ever could have imagined while sitting in front of that old Magnavox watching *Lassie*.

And guess what? Almost every day for lunch I now eat soup!

Starting a cookbook with 19 soup recipes might seem a little odd, but every one of these soups gives me a deep and instant sense of well-being. I hope they'll do the same for you. How much do I believe in the power of soup? Well, consider that the very best food advice I have to share comes down to this: If you want to feel warm and well-nourished—body and soul—find someone who looks like they could use a shot of goodness, and offer them a seat at your table, some easy conversation, and a simple bowl of soup. Because whoever you are, wherever you're from, there's no denying it: Soup is love.

SPICY BEAN AND COLLARD GREENS SOUP

My grandmother used to grow collard greens like weeds, which meant we either had collards or turnips at almost every meal. Adding collard greens to a plain bean soup takes it to a whole other dimension. Those greens spice everything up!

INGREDIENTS:

Beans

1 ½ cups dried cannellini or other small white beans, soaked overnight in water to cover by a few inches

½ medium yellow onion, chopped

3 cloves garlic, peeled and smashed

2 bay leaves

1 tablespoon kosher salt

For an easy and quick method use two 15-ounce cans of organic cannellini or other small white beans.

Soup

1 tablespoon extra virgin olive oil

½ medium yellow onion, chopped

1 rib celery, chopped

1 medium carrot, chopped

1 dried arbol chile

Salt

2 cloves garlic, minced

½ teaspoon red pepper flakes

1 tablespoon smoked paprika

4 cups Great Chicken Stock (page 42)

½ cup canned crushed tomatoes

½ teaspoon fresh thyme leaves

Freshly ground white pepper

4 large leaves collard greens, stems removed, chopped

1 tablespoon sherry vinegar or red wine vinegar

¼ cup finely grated Pecorino or Parmesan cheese

DIRECTIONS:

To cook the beans: Drain the beans. Combine the beans, onion, garlic, and bay leaves in a large saucepan and add cold water to cover by 2 inches. Bring to simmer over medium-high heat, add the salt, and reduce the heat to low. Cook until the beans are soft but not mushy, 35 to 40 minutes. Let the beans cool in their cooking liquid, then discard the bay leaves and drain.

To make the soup: In a large saucepan, heat the oil over medium-high heat. Add the onion, celery, carrot, arbol chile, and a large pinch of salt. Cook for about 5 minutes, until the vegetables are slightly softened and colored. Add the garlic, red pepper flakes, and smoked paprika and cook for about 30 seconds, stirring constantly, until aromatic. Stir in the beans, chicken stock, tomatoes, thyme, and a pinch of white pepper and bring to a boil. Reduce the heat to medium-low and simmer uncovered for 5 minutes. Remove the arbol chile.

Transfer 2 cups of the soup, including solids, to a blender and blend until smooth. Return the puree to the pan, add the collard greens, 1 teaspoon salt, and a little pepper, return to a simmer, and simmer for another 5 minutes, or until the collards are softened. Stir in the vinegar. Taste and add more salt if needed. Spoon into bowls and serve with the grated cheese on top.

PREP TIME	COOK TIME	SERVES	SMART POINTS	CALORIES
20 MINUTES	**65** MINUTES	**6**	**7** PER SERVING	**289** PER SERVING

MUSHROOM SOUP

We use a variety of different mushrooms, so it's chewy—really substantial without being heavy. Actually, for me this is every bit as filling as having a bowl of beef stew, but I don't feel so stuffed that I need a nap afterwards.

INGREDIENTS:

Extra virgin olive oil spray

4 ounces (about 2 cups) whole oyster mushrooms, cut in half if large

Salt

1 tablespoon extra virgin olive oil

1 medium yellow onion, finely chopped

1 clove garlic, minced

1 teaspoon dried thyme

1 pound button mushrooms, cleaned and sliced

1 bay leaf

3 cups Great Chicken Stock (page 42)

½ teaspoon freshly ground white pepper

¼ cup heavy cream

2 tablespoons grated Parmesan cheese

Freshly cracked black pepper

2 tablespoons chopped fresh parsley

DIRECTIONS:

Heat a large saucepan over medium heat and coat with cooking spray. Add the oyster mushrooms and a large pinch of salt and cook, stirring often, until slightly softened, about 5 minutes. Set aside.

Heat the oil over medium-low heat, add the onion, and cook until softened but not colored, about 5 minutes. Add the garlic and thyme and cook, stirring, for 1 minute. Add the button mushrooms, bay leaf, and 1 teaspoon salt, cover, and cook, stirring occasionally, for about 10 minutes, until the mushrooms are softened. Add the chicken stock and white pepper, cover again, raise the heat to high, and bring to a simmer. Reduce the heat to medium-low and cook for an additional 10 minutes. Add the cream and cook for a minute or so, until heated through. Remove the bay leaf.

Working in batches, transfer the soup to a blender and blend until smooth. Season with more salt if needed. Pour the soup into bowls and divide the oyster mushrooms among the bowls. Garnish with the cheese, cracked black pepper, and parsley, and serve.

PREP TIME	COOK TIME	SERVES	SmartPoints	CALORIES
10 MINUTES	30 MINUTES	4	6 PER SERVING	210 PER SERVING

The soup equivalent of wrapping yourself in a warm blanket—cozy, sensual, and perfect as a full meal.

HAWAIIAN BEAN AND VEGETABLE (OW RANCH) SOUP

A few years ago in Maui, we came across some huge lima beans that one of the farmers had harvested, dried, and stored in mason jars. Perfect for a soup! Originally, we used an oxtail base, something hearty enough to stand up to a big bean. But when I started on Weight Watchers, I realized that oxtail takes nearly a day's worth of points. So we developed a thick, rich, meatless base that's much lighter.

INGREDIENTS:

2 cups dried Christmas lima beans or cranberry beans (or substitute 6 cups canned lima beans, drained)

2 bay leaves

2 teaspoons salt

1 tablespoon extra virgin olive oil

1 small yellow onion, finely chopped

½ red bell pepper, cored, seeded, and finely chopped

3 medium ribs celery, finely chopped

2 medium carrots, finely chopped

2 cloves garlic, minced

2 tablespoons red pepper flakes

6 cups Great Chicken Stock (page 42)

1 strip orange peel, preferably dried, or 2 teaspoons orange zest

1 star anise

2-inch piece fresh ginger, very thinly sliced

¼ cup smooth unsweetened peanut butter

2 cups chopped mustard greens

Garnishes

Bean sprouts

Chopped fresh cilantro

Splash of lime juice

Sliced serrano chiles

Freshly grated ginger

Orange zest

Splash of sherry wine

DIRECTIONS:

If using dried beans, soak the beans in water to cover by a few inches for at least 8 hours or overnight. Drain the beans, then put them in a large saucepan along with 1 bay leaf. Add water to cover by a few inches and season lightly with salt. Bring to a boil over high heat, then reduce the heat and cook until softened, about 1 hour. Drain and remove the bay leaf. Transfer one-third of the cooked beans to a food processor or blender and puree them.

Rinse out and dry the pan, then add the oil and heat over medium-low heat. Add the onion, bell pepper, celery, carrots, and two teaspoons of salt and cook until the vegetables are softened but not colored, about 10 minutes. Add the garlic and red pepper flakes and cook until aromatic, about 2 minutes. Add the whole beans and bean puree, the chicken stock, orange peel, star anise, ginger, peanut butter, and the remaining bay leaf. Increase the heat to high and bring to a simmer, stirring to dissolve the bean puree and peanut butter, then reduce the heat and cook for 20 minutes. Add the mustard greens and cook for about 2 minutes, until wilted. Remove the orange peel, bay leaf, and star anise. Add the garnishes to individual soup bowls and pour the soup around them. Finish with a splash of sherry wine. Serve with small bowls of jasmine rice on the side.

PREP TIME	COOK TIME	SERVES	SMARTPOINTS	CALORIES
20 MINUTES	1 HOUR	6	8 PER SERVING	323 PER SERVING

MINESTRA VERDE

This is The Garden of Earthly Delights in a soup bowl. It's every
vegetable your mama told you to eat, but in this broth they're warm and
delicious and soothing and spicy—all at the same time.

INGREDIENTS:

8 sprigs fresh basil

4 sprigs fresh oregano

6 sprigs fresh thyme

1 tablespoon extra virgin olive oil

1 large yellow onion, finely chopped

1 large leek, white and green parts,
finely chopped

2 tablespoons minced garlic

Salt and freshly ground black pepper

2 large yellow or orange carrots, cut into
$\frac{1}{2}$-inch cubes

2 large ribs celery, cut into $\frac{1}{2}$-inch cubes

1 medium fennel bulb, cored and cut into
$\frac{1}{2}$-inch cubes

3 large green heirloom tomatoes

4 cups Great Chicken Stock or Vegetable
Stock (page 42)

2 bay leaves

2 cups cooked cannellini beans
(or one 15-ounce can, drained and rinsed)

4 cups loosely packed fresh spinach

2 tablespoons red wine vinegar, or to taste

1 cup chopped green beans,
cut into $\frac{1}{2}$-inch pieces

1 cup chopped asparagus, cut into $\frac{1}{2}$-inch pieces

1 small zucchini, cut into $\frac{1}{2}$-inch cubes

1 cup fresh or thawed frozen English peas

DIRECTIONS:

Tie the basil, oregano, and thyme together with
kitchen string to make an herb bundle.

In a large saucepan, heat the oil over medium-low
heat. Add the onion and leek and cook until softened
but not colored, about 10 minutes. Add the garlic
and cook for about 2 minutes, until aromatic. Season
with salt and pepper. Add the carrots, celery, fennel,
tomatoes, chicken or vegetable stock, herb bundle,
and bay leaves. Increase the heat to medium-high,
bring to a simmer, then reduce the heat and simmer
for about 15 minutes, until the vegetables are
softened. Add the beans, return to a simmer, and
cook for 5 minutes.

Remove 2 cups of the broth from the soup, pour
it into a blender, add the spinach, and blend until
smooth. Add the blended soup back to the pot and
add the vinegar. Return to a simmer, add the green
beans and asparagus, and cook for about 3 minutes,
until they are starting to soften. Add the zucchini
and cook for 1 minute, then add the peas and cook
for 1 final minute, or until all the vegetables are
tender. Taste and add more vinegar, salt, and/or
pepper if needed. Remove the herb bundle and bay
leaves, spoon into bowls, and serve.

PREP TIME	COOK TIME	SERVES	SMARTPOINTS	CALORIES
20	45	6	5	249
MINUTES	MINUTES		PER SERVING	PER SERVING

Did you know that artichokes have ZERO, as in nada, points?!

ARTICHOKE SOUP

We grow our own artichokes. It's a great big bushy plant, so you have to dig through a lot of green just to get that one artichoke. It's a big job, and knowing that really makes you appreciate what you're eating. The problem is, a person can only consume so many steamed artichokes in a lifetime. So one day I said, "Let's try them in a soup." The good news is the soup is delicious and artichokes have no fat at all— I mean, you can't get a much cleaner vegetable than the artichoke. The not-so-good news is that we can never have artichokes in the house without Stedman making the "Careful, you might choke!" joke. One of these days he'll forget to say it, and I'll have to check him for fever.

INGREDIENTS:

5 large artichokes

1 ½ tablespoons extra virgin olive oil

½ medium yellow onion, thinly sliced

Salt

2 large Yukon gold potatoes, peeled and diced

6 cups Great Chicken Stock (page 42)

Freshly ground white pepper

4 cups fresh spinach leaves

1 tablespoon fresh lemon juice, or to taste

DIRECTIONS:

Remove the hearts and bottoms from the artichokes and thinly slice them.

In a large saucepan, heat the oil over medium heat. Add the onion and artichokes, season lightly with salt, and cook until starting to soften, 5 to 7 minutes. Add the potatoes and stock, increase the heat to medium-high, cover the pot, and bring to a simmer. Reduce the heat to low and cook until the potatoes are very tender, about 10 minutes. Season with salt and pepper. Transfer half of the soup along with half of the spinach to a blender and blend until smooth. Repeat with the remaining vegetables, stock, and spinach, returning both to the pan and reheating if needed. Stir in the lemon juice, taste, and add more lemon juice, salt, and/or pepper if needed.

PREP TIME	COOK TIME	SERVES	SMARTPOINTS	CALORIES
25 MINUTES	**30** MINUTES	**6**	**6** PER SERVING	**283** PER SERVING

RED PEPPER, SAUSAGE, AND FENNEL SOUP

This soup is layered with flavors. And then the fennel just gives it a slight licorice kick.
Add a crunchy green salad and you'll feel *souper* satisfied!

INGREDIENTS:

1 large tomato, finely chopped

1 medium bulb fennel, cored and finely chopped

3 teaspoons extra virgin olive oil

Salt and freshly ground black pepper

1 large yellow onion, chopped

1 large carrot, chopped

1 large rib celery, chopped

3 cloves garlic, minced

1 bay leaf

4 cups Great Chicken Stock (page 42),
plus more if needed

1 (12-ounce) jar roasted red bell peppers, drained

2 spicy Italian chicken sausages, meat removed
from the casing

Leaves of ½ bunch Swiss chard, mustard greens,
or kale, chopped

½ teaspoon red pepper flakes

Optional garnishes

Chile olive oil

Grated Parmesan cheese

Cracked black pepper

Fresh basil leaves, cut into chiffonade

DIRECTIONS:

Preheat the oven to 300°F.

In a medium bowl, combine the tomato and fennel, stir in 1 teaspoon of the oil, and season with salt and pepper. Place on a small baking sheet (a pie plate works well), place in the oven, and roast for 40 minutes, or until the vegetables are softened. Remove from the oven and set aside.

Meanwhile, heat 1 teaspoon of the remaining oil in a large saucepan over medium-low heat. Add the onion, carrot, and celery and cook, stirring occasionally, until starting to soften but not browned, about 10 minutes. Add the garlic and bay leaf and cook for 1 minute, or until aromatic. Add the chicken stock, increase the heat to high, and bring to a simmer. Reduce the heat and simmer for 15 minutes, or until the vegetables are completely softened. Remove the bay leaf. Add the soup and roasted peppers to a blender and blend until smooth (do this in batches if necessary). Wipe out the saucepan and pour the soup back into it. Season with salt and pepper.

Heat the remaining 1 teaspoon oil in a large skillet over medium-high heat. Add the sausage and cook, stirring often, until well browned, about 5 minutes. Add the chard, greens, or kale and red pepper flakes and cook, stirring, until the greens are wilted, about 2 minutes.

To serve, spoon the soup into bowls, add the roasted tomatoes and fennel, then finish with the sausage and wilted greens and your choice of garnishes.

PREP TIME	COOK TIME	SERVES	SmartPoints	CALORIES
25 MINUTES	40 MINUTES	4	7 PER SERVING	339 PER SERVING

You can make this soup without any dairy and it tastes just as creamy.

SUMMER CORN CHOWDER

I bought a farm in Indiana almost 30 years ago, and that's when I first started a little corn patch. The thing is, every stalk grows so many ears that I couldn't keep up! I mean, what do you do with all that corn? When I was a kid, my mother used to fry it, which was great, but what made it so great was that she'd fry it in a pound of bacon. I began looking for some slightly less artery-clogging alternatives—that's when we came up with the corn chowder idea. By pureeing half of the corn and keeping the rest of the kernels whole, we were able to get a good, chunky chowder without having to dilute the flavor or thicken it by adding cream.

INGREDIENTS:

1 tablespoon unsalted butter

2 medium carrots, peeled and cut into small dice

1 medium yellow onion, cut into small dice

3 cloves garlic, thinly sliced

1 ½ teaspoons salt, plus more if needed

Kernels from 6 ears of corn, or 4 ½ cups thawed frozen corn kernels

1 medium baking potato, peeled and cut into small dice

6 cups Great Chicken Stock (page 42), plus more if needed

2 sprigs fresh thyme

1 bay leaf

½ cup canned evaporated milk

1 teaspoon freshly ground black pepper

Garnishes

4 thick slices great-quality bacon, cut into small dice

1 small sweet potato, peeled and cut into small dice

2 cups fresh or thawed frozen corn kernels

½ teaspoon ground chipotle chile

2 canned pimientos, drained and cut into small dice

2 tablespoons thinly sliced fresh chives

1 tablespoon finely chopped fresh tarragon

DIRECTIONS:

In a large, heavy-bottom saucepan, melt the butter over medium-low heat. Add the carrots, onion, garlic, and salt and cook for about 10 minutes, until softened but not browned. Add the corn and cook for 5 minutes more (if using frozen corn, no need to cook). Add the potato, chicken stock, thyme, and bay leaf, increase the heat to high, and bring to a boil. Reduce the heat and simmer for 20 minutes.

Meanwhile, prepare the garnishes: Cook the bacon in a large skillet over medium-high heat until crisp, about 5 minutes. Remove from the pan with a slotted spoon and drain on a paper towel–lined plate. Add the sweet potato to the pan and cook until browned and cooked through, about 8 minutes. Add the corn and chipotle and cook for 2 minutes more. Place the bacon in a medium bowl, add the sweet potato, corn, and pimientos, and toss in the chives and tarragon. Remove from the heat and set aside while you finish the soup.

Remove the bay leaf and thyme from the soup. With a mesh strainer or large slotted spoon, remove half of the solids from the pan and place in a blender. Add the evaporated milk, hold down the lid with a towel to avoid escaping steam, and blend until smooth. Return the puree to the pan and simmer for 5 minutes more. Add the pepper, taste, and add more salt if needed. Ladle into bowls, garnish with the sweet potato mixture, and serve.

PREP TIME	COOK TIME	SERVES	SmartPoints	CALORIES
30 MINUTES	1½ HOURS	8	9 PER SERVING	279 PER SERVING

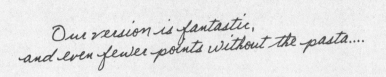

*One version is fantastic,
and even fewer points without the pasta....*

TUSCAN WHITE BEAN SOUP

I love Tuscany, and I love white beans. But I think it's the rosemary that always takes me back to the soup I had in Italy. That Pasta Fagioli was probably my favorite soup ever! We don't have the recipe in here because there is only one person who can make it. Her name is Nuncia, and she lives somewhere on the Italian coast.

INGREDIENTS:

2 cups dried cannellini beans (or substitute 6 cups canned beans, drained)

Sea salt

9 small tomatoes, cut in half

1 tablespoon extra virgin olive oil

Cracked black pepper

1 cup diced onion

1 bay leaf

1 cup diced carrots

1 cup diced celery

1 cup diced fennel

3 cloves garlic, minced

1 cup diced cremini mushrooms

2 cups reserved bean cooking liquid (or, if using canned beans, Great Chicken Stock, page 42), plus more if needed

8 large fresh basil leaves, cut into 1/4-inch strips

1/4 cup finely chopped fresh flat-leaf parsley

Optional garnishes

Chili oil

Grated Parmesan cheese

Cracked black pepper

DIRECTIONS:

If using dried beans, soak them in water to cover by a few inches for at least 8 hours or overnight. Drain and rinse the soaked beans. Place the beans in a large saucepan and add water to cover by 2 inches. Place over high heat and bring to a boil, then season with salt, reduce the heat to medium-low, and simmer for about 1 hour, until the beans are tender but still hold their shape. Strain the beans and reserve the cooking liquid.

Preheat the oven to 300°F.

Place the tomatoes in a medium bowl, add 1/2 tablespoon of the oil, and season lightly with salt and pepper. Toss to coat. Place the tomatoes cut side down onto a baking sheet, leaving 1 inch of space between each for their juices to release. Roast in the oven for 30 to 45 minutes, until the tomatoes are softened and wilted. Remove from the oven and set onto a cooling rack.

In a large skillet, heat the remaining 1/2 tablespoon oil over medium-high heat. Add the onions and bay leaf and cook for 1 minute. Add the carrots, celery, and fennel, season with salt, and cook for 3 to 5 minutes, until the vegetables just begin to soften. Add the garlic and mushrooms and cook until the mushrooms are softened and any liquid has evaporated, about 5 minutes. Remove the bay leaf and transfer the mixture to a medium saucepan.

Combine 1 cup of the cooked beans with the reserved bean liquid (or chicken stock if using canned beans) and blend until smooth. Stir into the soup pan, add the remaining beans, and stir to combine, adding more bean liquid if the soup is too thick. Divide the soup among bowls and top with the roasted tomatoes, basil, parsley, and any other garnishes you like.

PREP TIME	COOK TIME	SERVES	SMARTPOINTS	CALORIES
25 MINUTES	**1½** HOURS	**8**	**4** PER SERVING	**211** PER SERVING

TOMATO AND GUAJILLO CHILE SOUP

This is the best way to add a dash of cha-cha-cha to a simple tomato base.
If Timmy's mom hadn't been so committed to feeding him Campbell's every week,
this could've been a real treat! The guajillo balances the tomatoes
and keeps them from getting too acidic.

INGREDIENTS:

2 dried guajillo chiles

8 sprigs fresh cilantro

2 teaspoons extra virgin olive oil

1 small yellow onion, chopped

1 small carrot, chopped

2 cloves garlic, minced

¾ teaspoon sea salt, or to taste

½ teaspoon ground cumin

Kernels from 1 ear corn (about ¾ cup)

4 large ripe tomatoes, chopped

1 small jalapeño chile, seeded and
roughly chopped

½ cup cooked hominy

1 ½ teaspoons tomato paste

3 cups Great Chicken Stock or Vegetable Stock
(page 42)

Optional garnishes

Reserved cilantro leaves

Peeled and chopped cherry tomatoes

Shaved cabbage

Crema fresca

*As you may be noticing, I'm a
big fan of all things spicy.*

DIRECTIONS:

Heat a medium skillet over medium-high heat. Add the guajillo chiles and toast until darkened in color, about 1 minute, then flip them with tongs and toast for another minute or so, until darkened on the second side. Remove from the skillet, remove the stems, and shake out the seeds. Place the chiles in a medium bowl and add about 2 cups boiling water. Place a small plate on top of the chiles to keep them submerged and set aside to soak for about 20 minutes, until softened, then drain.

Separate the cilantro leaves and stems and chop the stems. Reserve the leaves for garnish.

In a large saucepan, heat the oil over medium-low heat. Add the onion, carrot, garlic, and salt and cook, stirring occasionally, until softened but not browned, about 10 minutes. Add the cumin and cook for about 1 minute, until fragrant. Add the corn and cook for 2 minutes, stirring often.

Meanwhile, combine the tomatoes, cilantro stems, guajillo and jalapeño chiles, hominy, tomato paste, and salt in the blender and puree until smooth, adding a little of the stock if needed to get the blender moving. Pour the puree into the soup pot, add the stock, place over medium-high heat, and bring to a simmer. Cover, reduce the heat to medium-low, and simmer for 15 minutes. Taste and add more salt if needed. Add choice of garnish and serve.

PREP TIME	COOK TIME	SERVES	SmartPoints	CALORIES
20 MINUTES	30 MINUTES	4	4 PER SERVING	173 PER SERVING

MULLIGATAWNY SOUP

I used to tape two, sometimes three, shows a day. I'd grab a little snack between tapings to keep my energy from flagging, then I'd come upstairs for some lunch at about 3:00. Mulligatawny was always one of my comfort soups. The diced apples and curry give it a slightly exotic flavor that you can't quite put your finger on—you just know it's wonderful.

INGREDIENTS:

1 tablespoon butter, ghee, or coconut oil

2 medium white onions, thinly sliced into half-moons

2 teaspoons salt

1 large Granny Smith apple, peeled, cored, and finely chopped

2-inch piece fresh ginger, grated

6 cloves garlic, chopped

2 teaspoons garam masala

2 tablespoons curry powder (I prefer Madras curry powder)

2 teaspoons ground coriander

2 teaspoons ground turmeric

1 teaspoon ground cumin

1 teaspoon ground cayenne

2 bay leaves

8 cups Great Chicken Stock or Vegetable Stock (page 42), plus more if needed

2 cups red lentils

2 (15-ounce) cans chickpeas

1 (14-ounce) can unsweetened lite coconut milk

Garnishes

1 small green apple, peeled, cored, and minced

½ cup finely chopped fresh cilantro

½ cup finely chopped scallions

Zest and juice of 1 lemon

DIRECTIONS:

Melt the butter, ghee, or coconut oil in a large saucepan over medium heat. Add the onions and salt and cook, stirring often, until the onions start to brown, about 15 minutes. Add the apple and continue to cook until the apple is completely softened and the onions are caramelized, another 10 to 15 minutes. Add the ginger, garlic, garam masala, curry powder, coriander, turmeric, cumin, cayenne, and bay leaves and sauté for 3 minutes, stirring often and adding a tiny bit of water if the mixture starts to stick.

Add the stock and lentils, bring to a simmer, then reduce the heat, cover, and simmer until the lentils begin to fall apart, 20 to 25 minutes.

While the soup is simmering, make the garnish: Combine the apple, cilantro, scallions, and lemon zest and juice and set aside for about 20 minutes, or until the soup is finished.

After the lentils begin to fall apart, you can either puree half of the soup and add it back to the pot, puree the whole thing, or leave it as is—it's up to you. Add the chickpeas and coconut milk, raise the heat briefly to bring the soup to a simmer, then lower the heat and simmer for 10 minutes, adding more stock if necessary for a thick but soupy consistency. If you reheat the soup the next day, you may need to add a little stock or water, as it tends to thicken further after it's been refrigerated.

PREP TIME	COOK TIME	SERVES	SMARTPOINTS	CALORIES
15 MINUTES	1½ HOURS	10	10 PER SERVING	327 PER SERVING

In the summer we take them fresh off the vine, and in the winter we roast them to concentrate the flavor when good tomatoes are almost impossible to find.

BASIC TOMATO SOUP

I've never met a tomato soup I didn't like. It looks rustic, it feels rich, and it tastes, well, honest. Here's a base that's beautiful just on its own—I like freezing a couple of batches to have on hand—and three vibrant garnish options on the following pages, if you feel like mixing things up a little.

INGREDIENTS:

1 tablespoon extra virgin olive oil

1 medium yellow onion, finely chopped

2 medium ribs celery, finely chopped

1 large carrot, finely chopped

6 medium fresh basil leaves, torn into pieces

Salt

3 cloves garlic, finely chopped

¼ cup tomato paste

6 large ripe tomatoes, peeled and chopped

3 cups Great Chicken Stock (page 42)

Freshly ground black pepper

Optional garnishes

Fresh basil leaves, cut into thin ribbons

Grated Parmesan cheese

Red pepper flakes

Tomato concassée
(peeled, seeded, and chopped tomato)

DIRECTIONS:

Heat the oil in a large saucepan over medium-low heat. Add the onion, celery, carrot, and basil. Season with salt, cover, and cook, stirring occasionally, until softened but not colored, 5 to 7 minutes. Add the garlic and cook for about 1 minute, until aromatic. Stir in the tomato paste and cook for 2 minutes, then add the tomatoes and chicken stock and season with salt and pepper. Increase the heat to high and bring to a simmer, then reduce the heat and simmer for 20 minutes to break down the tomatoes and blend the flavors.

Working in batches, pour the soup into a blender and blend until smooth (or leave part of it chunky for one of the variations), returning the soup to a new pan. Spoon into bowls and serve with your choice of garnish.

PREP TIME	COOK TIME	SERVES	SmartPoints	CALORIES
20 MINUTES	30 MINUTES	4	3 PER SERVING	165 PER SERVING

Soup Garnishes

Tomato soup makes a great base for lots of different kinds of toppings and garnishes. Here are a few of my favorites. But the truth is, you could add these to any soup you wanted. Especially the garlic croutons!

ROASTED GARLIC CROUTONS AND BASIL PUREE TOPPING

Croutons

6 large cloves garlic, peeled

1 tablespoon extra virgin olive oil

¼ teaspoon salt

8 (⅛-inch-thick) slices French baguette

Basil Puree

1 teaspoon salt

2 cups fresh basil leaves

2 tablespoons water

2 tablespoons extra virgin olive oil

To make the croutons: Preheat the oven to 350°F. In a small bowl, combine the garlic, oil, and salt. Place a double sheet of aluminum foil large enough to wrap around the garlic on a work surface. Transfer the garlic with its oil to the foil and fold the edges up to wrap the garlic into a packet. Place the packet in the oven and roast for 25 minutes, or until the garlic is completely softened and golden brown.

Place the sliced baguette on a small baking sheet and lightly dab it with the oil remaining around the garlic. Toast the slices until they are golden brown, about 10 minutes. Crush the remaining garlic with a fork and spread a thin layer over each crouton.

To make the basil puree: Fill a small bowl with water and ice to make an ice-water bath.

In a medium saucepan, bring 1 quart water to a boil. Add the salt and basil and blanch for 30 seconds, then drain and immediately transfer the basil to an ice bath. Drain again, squeezing out excess water. Place the basil in a blender, add the oil and two tablespoons of water, and blend until smooth.

To serve: Spoon the soup into bowls and top with 2 croutons and ½ teaspoon of the basil puree.

SERVES 4

4 SMARTPOINTS PER SERVING | 119 CALORIES

HEIRLOOM TOMATO SOUP WITH ZUCCHINI AND CORN

Basic Tomato Soup (see page 28), made with heirloom tomatoes
1 teaspoon extra virgin olive oil
1 teaspoon blackening spice
1 medium zucchini, cut into ¼-inch cubes
Kernels from 1 ear corn (¾ cup)
Salt

Make the soup according to the directions on page 28, but puree only half of the soup, leaving the rest chunky.

Heat the oil in a medium nonstick skillet over medium-high heat. Add the blackening spice and cook for a few seconds, until it sizzles. Add the zucchini and corn and cook, stirring often, until crisp-tender, about 3 minutes. Season with salt if needed. Spoon the soup into bowls and serve garnished with the corn and zucchini.

SERVES 4
4 SMARTPOINTS PER SERVING | 206 CALORIES

TOMATO SOUP WITH SAUTÉED MUSHROOMS AND GOAT CHEESE

Basic Tomato Soup (see page 28)
1 teaspoon extra virgin olive oil
2 cups cremini mushrooms, thinly sliced
4 teaspoons soft goat cheese, at room temperature
4 medium fresh basil leaves, cut into thin ribbons

Make the soup according to the directions on page 28, but puree only a quarter of the soup, leaving the rest chunky.

Heat the oil in a medium nonstick pan over medium heat. Add the mushrooms and sauté until softened, 5 to 7 minutes. Stir the mushrooms into the soup. Top each soup bowl with 1 teaspoon goat cheese and some of the basil ribbons.

SERVES 4
4 SMARTPOINTS PER SERVING | 197 CALORIES

For my favorite Skinny Cornbread go to page 56!

TURKEY CHILI

This is my go-to comfort food, but always with <u>cornbread.</u> We use only the dark meat of the turkey because it's more flavorful—and it feels as hearty as eating beef. By now, you may be noticing that I say, "The spicier, the better," where food is concerned. But only some like it hot, so I do have to temper it for other people. We always have a little side dish of chopped jalapeños or salsa or some serious red peppers at the table for me.

INGREDIENTS:

3 large dried guajillo chiles

1 large dried ancho chile

2 tablespoons extra virgin olive oil

1 pound ground dark meat turkey

1 medium yellow onion, chopped

½ medium red bell pepper, cored, seeded, and chopped

½ medium yellow bell pepper, cored, seeded, and chopped

2 ribs celery, chopped

2 jalapeño chiles, chopped

4 cloves garlic, minced

¼ cup chili powder

2 tablespoons ground cumin

1 tablespoon ground coriander

1 teaspoon ground cayenne

1 (28-ounce) can diced tomatoes, with juices

2 cups Great Chicken Broth (page 42)

2 bay leaves

1 teaspoon salt, plus more to taste

2 (15-ounce) cans red kidney beans, rinsed and drained

Optional garnishes

Sliced scallions

Grated cheddar cheese

Crumbled cotija cheese

Lime wedges

Sour cream or crème fraîche

Chopped fresh cilantro

DIRECTIONS:

Heat a medium skillet over medium-high heat. Add the guajillo and ancho chiles and toast until darkened in color, about 1 minute, then flip them with tongs and toast for another minute or so, until darkened on the second side. Remove from the skillet, remove the stems, and shake out the seeds. Place the chiles in a medium bowl and add 2 cups boiling water. Place a small plate on top of the chiles to keep them submerged and set aside to soak for about 20 minutes, until softened, then transfer to a blender and blend until smooth.

In a large, heavy-bottom saucepan, heat the oil over medium-high heat. Add the turkey and cook, stirring to break up any clumps, until lightly browned, about 5 minutes. Add the onion, bell peppers, celery, and jalapeños and cook for about 10 minutes, until the vegetables are softened. Add the garlic and cook for about 1 minute, until softened. Add the chili powder, cumin, coriander, and cayenne and cook, stirring to blend well, for 1 minute. Add the tomatoes, chicken broth, dried chile puree, bay leaves, and salt and bring to a boil. Reduce the heat and simmer, stirring occasionally, for about 30 minutes, until thickened. Add the beans and cook, stirring occasionally, for 10 minutes longer. Spoon into bowls and serve with your choice of toppings.

PREP TIME	COOK TIME	SERVES	SmartPoints	CALORIES
30	40	8	6	264
MINUTES	MINUTES		PER SERVING	PER SERVING

For an extra tasty twist to this recipe, try barbecuing the shrimp!

SPRING PEA SOUP WITH GRILLED SHRIMP

I *looove* peas! The only vegetable I love even more is the potato. I love potatoes so much
that I once attempted to make a potato cocktail. Anyway, I eat potatoes sparingly and
green peas come in a very close second on the favorites list—so this soup is a regular at my house.
The grilled shrimp turns it into a protein-packed lunch.

INGREDIENTS:

Shrimp

1 teaspoon grapeseed oil

½ teaspoon sea salt

½ teaspoon ground chipotle chile

1 teaspoon agave nectar

16 large shrimp (about 12 ounces),
peeled and deveined

Zest of 1 lemon

2 tablespoons thinly sliced fresh chives

Soup

1 tablespoon extra virgin olive oil

2 leeks, white and light green parts, sliced

1 teaspoon sea salt, or to taste

1 shallot, minced

2 cloves garlic, smashed and peeled

3 cups Great Chicken Stock (page 42),
plus more if needed

4 cups fresh or thawed frozen peas

1 cup buttermilk

⅓ cup chopped fresh basil leaves

2 tablespoons chopped fresh
tarragon leaves

½ teaspoon freshly ground black pepper

2 tablespoons crème fraîche

DIRECTIONS:

Marinate the shrimp: In a large bowl, mix the grapeseed
oil, salt, chipotle powder, and agave into a paste. Add the
shrimp and stir to coat. Cover and place in the refrigerator
while you prepare the soup.

Make the soup: Heat the olive oil in a large saucepan over
medium-low heat. Add the leeks and ½ teaspoon of the salt
and cook for 8 minutes, or until softened. Add the shallot and
garlic and sauté for 4 minutes more, or until softened. Add
the chicken stock and the remaining ½ teaspoon salt, raise
the heat briefly to bring it to a simmer, then lower the heat
and simmer for 20 minutes. Add the peas and cook for 3 to 5
minutes, until they are tender.

Strain the soup into another saucepan. Place the solids in
a blender along with the buttermilk, basil, and tarragon
and blend until smooth. If necessary, ladle some of the
broth into the blender (carefully, as it will be hot) until
you have a smooth puree. Slowly add the puree back into
the pot with the broth. Add the pepper, taste, and add
more salt if needed. Keep warm over very low heat while
you prepare the shrimp.

Make the shrimp: Heat a grill or grill pan over medium-
high heat. Remove the shrimp from the refrigerator. Place
the shrimp on the pan in one layer and cook until pink,
about 3 minutes on each side. Move the shrimp to a bowl
and stir in the lemon zest and chives. Pour the soup into
bowls and slightly swirl 1 ½ teaspoons of crème fraîche in
each (do not mix it in completely). Arrange 4 shrimp into
the middle of each bowl and serve.

What can I say? It seemed like a good idea at the time, but it turns out the only way to drink a potato is when its distilled into vodka.

PREP TIME	COOK TIME	SERVES	SMARTPOINTS	CALORIES
15 MINUTES	1 HOUR	4	10 PER SERVING	387 PER SERVING

The producers never called back but I made the broccoli soup again and again.

BROCCOLI SOUP WITH CASHEW CREAM

My first memory of this soup goes back to around 1978. I was asked to do a tiny walk-on part, playing myself, on *All My Children*. Needless to say, I wanted to lose some weight before heading to "Pine Valley," so I began boiling broccoli in chicken broth and then pureeing it. I'd have it every day, all in an effort to look thin when I uttered the immortal line, "Excuse me, aren't you Pamela Kingsley?"

INGREDIENTS:

1 tablespoon extra virgin olive oil

1 medium yellow onion, diced

1 large head broccoli, florets cut into 1-inch pieces, stems peeled and diced

2 cloves garlic, minced

¼ cup white wine

4 cups Great Chicken Stock (page 42)

1 bay leaf

Salt and freshly ground black pepper

Cashew Cream

It was years later that I was introduced to the luxury of cashew cream.

DIRECTIONS:

Heat the oil in a Dutch oven or large saucepan over medium heat. Add the onion and cook for 3 minutes, or until starting to soften. Add the broccoli stems and cook for another 5 minutes, or until softened. Add the garlic and cook for about 1 minute, until aromatic, then add the wine and cook, stirring, for another minute. Add the chicken stock, increase the heat to high, and bring to a simmer. Add the broccoli florets and bay leaf, return to a simmer, then lower the heat and cook until the broccoli is tender, 5 to 7 minutes. Remove the bay leaf and season with salt and pepper. Working in batches, transfer the soup to a blender and blend until smooth, returning each batch to the pot as it's done. Taste and adjust the seasonings as needed and reheat if needed. Spoon into bowls and top each bowl with 1 tablespoon of the cashew cream.

Cashew Cream

1 cup raw cashews

Place the cashews in a medium bowl, add cold water to cover by a couple of inches, cover with a kitchen towel, and set aside on the counter for 3 to 4 hours. Drain, then transfer the cashews to a blender, add ½ cup fresh cold water, and blend until smooth. The cream can be stored in a covered container in the refrigerator for up to a week.

PREP TIME	COOK TIME	SERVES	SMARTPOINTS	CALORIES
5 MINUTES	20 MINUTES	4	5 PER SERVING	239 PER SERVING

FRENCH GREEN LENTIL SOUP

I love this soup because lentils are packed with protein and minerals—
they're one of the healthiest foods you can eat.

INGREDIENTS:

Tomato Concassée (concassée is peeled, seeded, and chopped tomatoes)

1 medium tomato, peeled, seeded, and finely diced

1 small clove garlic, minced

1 teaspoon extra virgin olive oil

Dash of balsamic vinegar

1 fresh basil leaf, chopped

Pinch of salt and pepper

Soup

10 sprigs fresh thyme

2 bay leaves

Salt

2 cups French green lentils

1 tablespoon extra virgin olive oil

½ cup finely chopped yellow onion

½ cup finely chopped celery

3 cloves garlic, grated on a Microplane (page 218)

1 to 2 serrano chiles, seeded and chopped

5 cups Great Chicken Stock (page 42), plus more if needed

Freshly ground black pepper

½ cup tomato concassée

Add some spice with a jalapeño or two!

DIRECTIONS:

To make the tomato concassée: Combine all the ingredients in a small bowl and let sit while you make the soup.

To make the soup: Make an herb sachet by using kitchen string to tie the thyme with the bay leaves. Bring a large saucepan of water to a boil over high heat. Salt the water, then add the lentils and return to a boil. Drain the lentils and rinse them under cold water.

Rinse out the pot, dry it, then add the oil and heat over medium-low heat. Add the onion, celery, garlic, and chiles, cover, and cook for 4 minutes, lifting the lid a couple of times to stir, until the vegetables are softened but not browned. Add the lentils and chicken stock, increase the heat to high, and bring to a simmer. Add the herb sachet, reduce the heat to medium-low, and simmer for about 30 minutes, until the lentils are tender. Season with salt and pepper. Transfer a quarter of the soup to a blender and blend until smooth. Return the puréed soup to the pot, spoon into bowls, top each with some of the tomato concassée, and serve.

PREP TIME	COOK TIME	SERVES	SMARTPOINTS	CALORIES
10 MINUTES	30 MINUTES	8	7 PER SERVING	258 PER SERVING

This is one of my favorite winter soups. Filling and delicious, even without the cheese!

38

KALE AND FARRO SOUP

I like all things grain: barley, grits, farro—you name it. When that diet came out that said
wheat was bad for you, I was like, "Well, I'm in big trouble, cause that's what my body craves."
And let's face it: Kale is the new black! We use it in a lot of soups.

INGREDIENTS:

1 tablespoon extra virgin olive oil

1 small yellow onion, finely chopped

1 leek, white and light green parts, thinly sliced

2 medium carrots, diced

2 ribs celery, diced

2 cloves garlic, finely chopped

2 cups pearled farro, rinsed and drained

6 cups Great Chicken Stock (page 42)

2 cups peeled butternut squash,
cut into 1/2-inch cubes

1 (14-ounce) can diced tomatoes, with juices

2- to 3-inch Parmesan cheese rind

1 bay leaf

1 teaspoon dried thyme

1 1/2 teaspoons salt, or to taste

1/2 teaspoon freshly ground black pepper,
or to taste

1 bunch kale, stems removed and
coarsely chopped

Finely grated Parmesan cheese

DIRECTIONS:

Heat the oil in a large saucepan over medium heat.
Add the onion and leek and cook until softened but
not colored, about 4 minutes. Add the carrots and
celery and cook for another 4 minutes, or until they
are starting to soften. Add the garlic and cook until
fragrant, about 1 minute. Add the farro and stir
to coat. Add the chicken stock, squash, tomatoes,
cheese rind, bay leaf, thyme, salt, and pepper.
Increase the heat to high, bring to a simmer, then
reduce the heat to medium-low, partially cover
the pot, and simmer until the squash and farro are
tender, 30 to 40 minutes. Stir in the kale leaves and
simmer for 2 minutes, or until softened. Remove
and discard the cheese rind and bay leaf. Taste
and add more salt and pepper if needed. Spoon
into bowls, sprinkle each with about 1 tablespoon
Parmesan, and serve.

Not just in soups, either! See page 179 for a Kale Chip recipe with no points.

PREP TIME	COOK TIME	SERVES	SMARTPOINTS	CALORIES
20 MINUTES	45 MINUTES	6	10 PER SERVING	416 PER SERVING

YOUNG GARLIC SOUP

Unless you're trying to scare a vampire off, I have a feeling most people aren't exactly longing
for a bowl of garlic soup. I was a little skeptical myself, but we grow the garlic in the garden
and pick it before it's fully matured. Then we blanch it, to pull out any sting or bitterness.
What you have left is a silky-smooth soup that's light and luscious.

INGREDIENTS:

1 tablespoon extra virgin olive oil

8 ounces young spring garlic, roots and tops
trimmed, using the white part and about 2
inches of the light green part (about 4)

1 medium yellow onion, sliced into half-moons

1 large leek, white and light green parts, sliced

Salt and freshly ground white pepper

4 cloves garlic, minced

4 cups Great Chicken Stock (page 42),
plus more if needed

1 pound Yukon gold potatoes,
peeled and chopped

½ cup Cashew Cream (page 36)

2 cups baby spinach leaves

1 tablespoon fresh lemon juice, or to taste

Optional garnishes

Sautéed spring garlic

Garlic flowers

Finely chopped fresh chives

Splash of extra virgin olive oil

DIRECTIONS:

Heat the oil in a large saucepan over medium-low
heat. Add the spring garlic, onion, and leek and
season with salt and white pepper. Cook, stirring
occasionally, until the vegetables are softened but
not colored, about 10 minutes. Add the garlic and
cook for about 1 minute, until aromatic. Add the
chicken stock and potatoes, increase the heat to
medium-high, and bring just to a simmer. Reduce
the heat to medium-low and simmer until the
potatoes are cooked through, about 15 minutes,
watching the pan carefully so the soup doesn't reach
a boil at any point.

Transfer the soup in batches to a blender and
blend until smooth, adding the cashew cream and
spinach with the last batch. Return to the pan and
stir to combine, adding more stock if the soup is too
thick. Add the lemon juice, taste, and add more salt,
pepper, and/or lemon juice if needed. Rewarm the
soup if needed, or cool completely, refrigerate, and
serve chilled. Spoon into bowls and serve with your
choice of garnishes.

PREP TIME	COOK TIME	SERVES	SMARTPOINTS	CALORIES
20 MINUTES	15 MINUTES	4	9 PER SERVING	331 PER SERVING

GREAT CHICKEN STOCK

INGREDIENTS:

3 pounds chicken wings, legs, and backs

1 medium yellow onion, chopped

3 whole cloves garlic, peeled

1 bay leaf

½ teaspoon salt

DIRECTIONS:

Remove the skin and fat from the chicken and cut the chicken into 2-inch pieces. In a stockpot, combine all the ingredients. Add enough water to cover by 2 inches (about 3 quarts). Bring to a boil over high heat, skimming any foam that rises to the top. Reduce the heat to low and cook uncovered at a low simmer for 3 hours, topping the pot off with simmering water if it starts to get low. Remove from the heat, strain through a colander, and discard the solids. Let the stock cool completely, then skim off and discard the fat layer and pour into containers. The stock will keep for up to 3 days in the refrigerator or up to 3 months in the freezer.

PREP TIME	COOK TIME	SERVES	SmartPoints	CALORIES
5	3	10	3	86
MINUTES	HOURS	MAKES ABOUT 10 CUPS	PER SERVING	PER SERVING

VEGETABLE STOCK

INGREDIENTS:

2 medium onions, chopped

2 leeks, including dark green parts, sliced and rinsed well

3 large carrots, sliced

3 ribs celery, sliced

10 cloves garlic, peeled and smashed

1 teaspoon extra virgin olive oil

1 teaspoon sea salt

1 medium turnip, chopped

2 medium parsnips, chopped

2 medium tomatoes, chopped

2 bay leaves

5 sprigs fresh thyme

1 teaspoon black peppercorns

1 cup roughly chopped fresh parsley

12 cups water

DIRECTIONS:

Combine the onions, leeks, carrots, celery, garlic, oil, and salt in a large Dutch oven or stockpot. Cover and cook over medium-low heat for about 20 minutes, stirring occasionally, until the vegetables are softened but not browned. Add the remaining ingredients, including the water, increase the heat to high, partially cover the pan, and bring to a simmer. Reduce the heat to maintain a low simmer and cook for 1 hour. Remove from the heat and strain the broth through a fine-mesh sieve without pressing on the solids. Discard the solids. Let the stock cool completely, then pour into containers. The stock will keep for up to 4 days in the refrigerator or up to 1 month in the freezer.

PREP TIME	COOK TIME	SERVES	SmartPoints	CALORIES
30	80	10	2	89
MINUTES	MINUTES	MAKES ABOUT 10 CUPS	PER SERVING	PER SERVING

"WHEN YOU INVITE PEOPLE TO YOUR HOME, YOU INVITE THEM TO YOURSELF."
—OPRAH WINFREY

CHAPTER

2

WHAT ARE YOU *REALLY* HUNGRY FOR?

BACK WHEN I WAS JUST STARTING OUT AT WJZ-TV IN BALTIMORE,

I had a body I liked (130 pounds on the dot) and a colleague and soon-to-be best friend forever (for real) named Gayle King. Unfortunately, I also had a powerful need to please everybody on a never-ending basis, and a shopping mall complete with a big fast food court located directly across from my apartment. After a full day of covering stories that often left me depleted, and saying yes when I needed to say no, I'd prowl that food court, starting at one end with a cheese-and-bacon baked potato and finishing at the other with a giant chocolate chip macadamia nut cookie. When the scale registered 140, I took myself to a diet doctor.

The pills he put me on made me crazy; my mouth went dry, my heart pounded furiously. I couldn't sleep, I couldn't think, and I definitely couldn't keep taking those pills. What I could do was continue dropping by the food court.

By the time I left Maryland for Chicago, in 1984, I was eight years older and 42 pounds heavier than when I'd arrived. I vowed to use the move as a fresh start: Whoever tuned in to watch me host *A.M. Chicago* would see a woman who'd gotten serious about losing weight. There was just one problem: The more I dieted the more I gained, and the more I gained the more I ate.

But while I was gaining weight, my career was gaining traction. I was even invited to appear on *The Tonight Show*—my national television debut. Wow! The date was marked on my family's calendars, the plane ride was first-class, the hotel was five stars, California was sunny, Joan Rivers was guest hosting, and I was ready!

Joan's introduction is great. I make it from curtain to couch without tripping—so far, so good. I launch into my amusing little anecdote about winning the Miss Fire Prevention pageant, it's all going smoothly, I'm starting to settle in, and then it happens: Joan Rivers interrupts with perhaps the only question I haven't prepared for: "So how'd you gain the weight?"

Miss Fire Prevention, 1972

Wait a minute—did she just use my national television debut to ask me why I was so fat? The studio started spinning. The word fat...fat... FAAAAT reverberated in my brain. Joan sat behind Johnny's big wooden desk, telling me that she didn't want to hear my excuses and that I shouldn't have let this happen. The audience laughed nervously as she wagged her flawlessly manicured finger at me, pointed out that I was still "a single girl," and challenged me to come back 15 pounds lighter next time she hosted. And the whole time I just sat there smiling breezily, wanting nothing more than to crawl under my chair.

Naturally, I went home to Chicago and started planning my next big diet, the one that would get Joan and the rest of America to...what? Finally be impressed? Validate me, respect me, welcome me with open arms? If all I had to do to make everybody realize how deserving I was of my success—how worthy I was of approval—was lose 15 pounds, then let the dieting begin! Again!

And so it went. Eventually, I would try them all: The Cabbage Soup Diet, The Grapefruit Diet, The South Beach Diet, The Scarsdale Diet, The Atkins Diet, The I-Don't-Care-What-You've-Gotta-Do-To-Fit-Into-That-Vera-Wang-Dress Diet, The Liquid Diet, The Beverly Hills All-Fruit Diet. You name it—I've skinned, peeled, seeded, or juice-cleansed it.

The maddening part was, I was pretty good at diets. I could get the weight off—I just couldn't keep it off. And when it inevitably returned, it always brought some extra along for the ride—a ride that didn't end until I hit 237 deeply frustrating pounds.

If you asked me why I ate, I'd have forced a laugh and said it was because I loved food. But lots of people love food without crossing into obesity. So what was it, then? What was I really hungry for?

Gayle King was, is, and will always be my best friend forever.

Soon after I started hosting AM Chicago, our viewers started calling it The Oprah Show—hence the name change.

The fridge and I have been at odds for years. Now we're in daily peace talks.

Stedman Graham is, among many, many other things, my favorite person to cook for!

There was a night about two months into my now infamous four-month fast when I came home ready to forget the whole friggin' diet and eat anything within reach. There I stood in the kitchen, ogling Stedman's leftovers, when he walked in, saw I was ready to give up, and said, "Come here and let me give you a hug." In that moment, I needed nothing more.

I believe Bruce Springsteen got it right: "Everybody has a hungry heart." And maybe we're all just looking to fill up on a large helping of uncomplicated, unconditional love. When I was a girl, there wasn't always enough of that to go around. But as an adult I came to realize that even when people have the time and strength to care for you, the deepest care must ultimately come from your own self-acceptance, self-respect, and hard-earned truth. When I feel emotionally depleted or deprived, when I'm overwhelmed by life's pressures, food has always been my drug of choice—the way alcohol or gambling or shopping might be for someone else. But none of these are fixes. They're all just empty promises. They don't actually fill you up inside. They're like junk food for your soul.

When I manage to nourish myself with the stuff that really matters, food tends to be much less complicated. These are the moments when I'm just genuinely hungry for a wonderful meal, a good sipping tequila, and a long talk with a couple of old friends.

The recipes included in this chapter lend themselves to wonderful meals, for sure. They're like comfort-food makeovers, redesigned to be healthier versions of their former selves. Smothered chicken is now not so smothered, lasagna features thinly sliced veggies instead of pasta, and even Art Smith's amazing fried chicken recipe has been retooled to save some calories. I don't know about cake, but it turns out you can have your mashed potatoes and eat 'em, too!

MASHED CAULI-POTATOES

Everybody always says that whipped cauliflower tastes just like mashed potatoes. Well, guess what? Whipped cauliflower tastes just like...whipped cauliflower. So I was just staring at my plate of cauliflower one day and I started thinking: What if instead of pureeing a head of cauliflower and trying to fake yourself out, you were to mix in a potato or two? It turns out the cauliflower takes on the flavor of the potato. Who'd have thunk it? People have eaten the cauliflower mashed potato combination at my house, never even realizing the cauliflower was there. It makes you feel like you've actually beaten the system!

INGREDIENTS:

1 medium head white or golden cauliflower

Sea salt

2 medium Yukon gold potatoes, peeled and cut in half

1 tablespoon butter

1 teaspoon freshly ground black pepper

1 tablespoon finely chopped fresh rosemary

1 tablespoon finely chopped fresh chives

I love mashed potatoes, but if I eat too much, they don't love me back.

DIRECTIONS:

Remove the stem and outer leaves from the cauliflower and break the head into 8 to 10 sections.

Fill a large saucepan with water and season generously with salt. Add the potatoes, turn the heat to high, and bring to a boil. Reduce the heat to maintain a strong simmer and cook for 10 to 15 minutes, until the potatoes are tender. Using a slotted spoon, transfer the potatoes from the water to a colander. Add the cauliflower to the water, return to a simmer, and cook for 7 to 10 minutes, until tender. Remove the cauliflower from the pot and add it to the potatoes. Drain the water and return the potatoes and cauliflower to the pot. Add the butter, pepper, and rosemary and mash using a potato masher to a coarse mashed-potato texture. Season with salt and serve garnished with the chives.

PREP TIME	COOK TIME	SERVES	SmartPoints	CALORIES
10 MINUTES	15 MINUTES	6	2 PER SERVING	98 PER SERVING

MAYA'S SMOTHERED CHICKEN

My dear friend Maya Angelou made this when I visited her in North Carolina.
Maya was an extraordinary cook. No matter what she made, it always felt like coming home to
visit my grandmother, but this was my all-time favorite.

INGREDIENTS:

2 (3-pound) fryer chickens

Juice of 2 lemons

½ cup (1 stick) unsalted butter

½ cup vegetable oil, plus more if needed

½ teaspoon salt, plus more to taste

½ teaspoon freshly ground black pepper,
plus more to taste

1 cup all-purpose flour

2 medium onions, sliced

1 pound button mushrooms, sliced

1 clove garlic, minced

2 cups Great Chicken Stock (page 42)

DIRECTIONS:

Wash and pat dry the chicken with paper towels. Cut up each one into pieces and put them in a large bowl. Add the lemon juice, then add water to cover. Refrigerate for 1 hour.

Melt the butter in the oil in a large skillet over high heat.

Drain the chicken, pat it dry with paper towels, and season with the salt and pepper. Place ¾ cup of the flour in a shallow bowl. In batches, dredge the chicken pieces in the flour, shaking off any excess flour.

Working in batches, add the chicken pieces to the skillet and cook until the skin is browned and crisp, about 5 minutes on each side, removing the chicken from the skillet to a plate or baking sheet as it is finished and adding more oil if it starts to get low.

Measure out ¼ cup of the fat from the pan and pour it into a large saucepan. Heat over medium heat, then add the remaining ¼ cup flour and cook, stirring constantly, until a light brown roux is formed, about 5 minutes. Add the onions, mushrooms, and garlic and cook, stirring constantly and scraping the bottom of the pan as needed, until softened, about 10 minutes. Return the chicken to the pan and add the chicken stock. Increase the heat to high, bring to a simmer, then reduce the heat and simmer, stirring often to release any stuck bits from the bottom of the pan, for 25 minutes, or until the chicken is cooked through and the gravy has thickened enough to coat a spoon. Season with salt and pepper and serve.

This is the meal I remember most from childhood. My grandmother made it and served it over steaming rice when Sunday "company" came for dinner.

PREP TIME	COOK TIME	SERVES	SMARTPOINTS	CALORIES
15 MINUTES	50 MINUTES	8	15 PER SERVING	536 PER SERVING

MY SMOTHERED CHICKEN (REDUCED POINTS)

RECIPE COURTESY OF CHEF KENNY GILBERT

I wondered if there was a way to make Maya's smothered chicken not so...smothered. There is!
Instead of gravy loaded with flour and butter, we liquefy the onion, so the sauce is
vegetable-based. If the kitchen window is open, you can smell it cooking when you enter the yard.

This dish smells like Sundays and the feeling of sitting down to grace.

INGREDIENTS:

Roasted chicken

16 chicken drumsticks

1 tablespoon vegetable oil

1 tablespoon celery seed

1 tablespoon ground coriander

1 tablespoon red pepper flakes

1 tablespoon kosher salt

1 tablespoon ground black pepper

Braising liquid

1 quart Great Chicken Stock (page 42)

1 teaspoon vegetable oil

1 cup diced onion

1 cup diced carrot

1 cup diced celery

1 tablespoon celery seed

1 tablespoon ground coriander

1 tablespoon kosher salt

1 teaspoon crushed red pepper flakes

1 teaspoon ground black pepper

2 bay leaves

2 teaspoons chopped fresh thyme

DIRECTIONS:

To roast the chicken: Preheat the oven to 500°F.
Put the chicken in a large bowl and toss with the oil.
In a small bowl, combine the celery seed, coriander,
red pepper flakes, salt, and black pepper. Add to the
chicken and toss to coat. Place on a baking sheet and
bake for 15 to 20 minutes, turning once, until the legs
are starting to brown. Remove the chicken from the
oven and reduce the oven temperature to 300°F.

**While the chicken is roasting, make the braising
liquid:** Pour the chicken stock into a medium
saucepan. Place over medium heat, and heat until
hot, but don't let it come to a boil. Heat the oil in a
medium sauté pan over medium-high heat. Add the
remaining ingredients and sauté until the vegetables
are softened, about 5 minutes. Remove the bay leaves
and transfer the vegetables to a blender. Add the hot
chicken stock and blend until smooth.

To smother the chicken: Transfer the legs to a
large roasting dish. Pour the braising liquid over the
chicken legs, cover with aluminum foil, and bake
for 60 to 75 minutes, until the sauce is bubbling and
thick enough to coat a spoon. Remove the chicken
from the oven, let rest for 10 minutes, and serve, over
brown rice if you like. The chicken will keep in the
refrigerator for up to 3 days.

PREP TIME	COOK TIME	SERVES	SMARTPOINTS	CALORIES
15	80		8	390
MINUTES	MINUTES		PER SERVING	PER SERVING

It's also pretty great alongside a bowl of turkey chili.

SKINNY CORNBREAD

I want to feel great. I want to look good. But I draw the line at giving up cornbread. Fortunately, I don't like it real thick. My cornbread is thin and crispy right around the rim. I like when the edges sort of crunch in your mouth and there's a little bit of corn and jalapeño in there.

INGREDIENTS:

Extra virgin olive oil cooking spray

¼ cup diced yellow onion

½ cup fresh or thawed frozen corn kernels

2 tablespoons seeded and finely diced jalapeño chiles

½ cup all-purpose flour

2 teaspoons sugar

2 teaspoons baking powder

¼ teaspoon baking soda

½ teaspoon fine sea salt

1 cup stone-ground yellow cornmeal

¾ cup buttermilk

1 large egg, beaten

2 tablespoons grapeseed oil

DIRECTIONS:

Preheat the oven to 400°F. Coat a small nonstick skillet with cooking spray and heat over medium-high heat. Add the onion, corn, and jalapeños and cook until the corn is slightly charred, about 5 minutes. Transfer the vegetables to a bowl and set aside to cool to room temperature.

Sift the flour, sugar, baking powder, baking soda, and salt into a medium bowl. Add the cornmeal and whisk to blend the ingredients.

In a separate medium bowl, whisk together the buttermilk, egg, and oil. Pour the wet ingredients into the dry ingredients and stir with a wooden spoon to combine. Fold in the corn mixture.

Coat a 10-inch cast-iron skillet with cooking spray and pour the cornbread mixture into the pan. Level and smooth the top with a metal spatula. Place in the oven and bake for 15 minutes, or until lightly golden and the top center is just firm to the touch. Remove from the oven and set the skillet onto a cooling rack or trivet. Cool slightly, then slice and serve while still warm. The cornbread will keep, wrapped in plastic wrap, in the refrigerator for up to 1 week.

PREP TIME	COOK TIME	SERVES	SMARTPOINTS	CALORIES
15	15	8	5	152
MINUTES	MINUTES		PER SERVING	PER SERVING

If you have leftover cornbread it can be diced and dried in the oven for amazing croutons.

ART SMITH'S BUTTERMILK FRIED CHICKEN

Art Smith fries his chicken for people all over the world. He's made it for the Palestinians and the Israelis, he's even made it in Tiananmen Square. Apparently, the only thing everyone on the planet can agree on is Art's fried chicken is some of the best in the world.

INGREDIENTS:

Brine
1 gallon cold water
½ cup kosher salt
1 teaspoon black peppercorns
3 sprigs fresh rosemary
5 sprigs fresh thyme
4 cloves garlic, smashed and peeled
2 bay leaves

Chicken
2 (3½- to 4-pound) chickens, cut into 10 pieces
1 quart buttermilk
Canola oil

Egg wash
6 large eggs
1 tablespoon hot sauce
2 teaspoons table salt
2 teaspoons ground black pepper

Dredge
2 cups all-purpose flour
3 cups self-rising flour
1 tablespoon garlic powder
1 tablespoon onion powder
1 tablespoon table salt
2 tablespoons paprika
½ teaspoon ground cayenne
2 teaspoons dried thyme

DIRECTIONS:

To make the brine: In a stockpot, combine 2 cups of the water with the salt. Place over medium-high heat and bring to a boil, stirring to dissolve the salt. Add the remaining water along with the black peppercorns, rosemary, thyme, garlic, and bay leaves. Transfer to a container large enough to hold the chicken and brine together.

To prepare the chicken: Place the chicken pieces in the brine, cover, and refrigerate for at least 12 hours. Remove the chicken from the brine, shaking off any spices that may have stuck to it. Pour the brine out of the container, add the buttermilk, and submerge the chicken in the buttermilk. Cover and refrigerate for 4 to 6 hours.

To make the egg wash: In a very large bowl, whisk together the eggs, hot sauce, salt, and pepper. Drain the chicken pieces from the buttermilk and put them in the bowl with the egg wash, turning the pieces to coat them completely.

To make the dredge: In a large bowl, whisk together the all-purpose flour, self-rising flour, garlic powder, onion powder, salt, paprika, cayenne, and thyme. Spread the mixture out in a large shallow bowl or on a baking sheet. Remove two pieces of chicken at a time from the egg wash, letting excess liquid drain off. Roll in the seasoned flour, shake off any excess flour (this is important for successful frying), and lay the chicken on a wire rack. Repeat with the remaining chicken pieces.

To fry the chicken: Pour oil into a large cast-iron skillet to come 1 inch up the sides. Heat over medium heat until it registers 325°F on a deep-frying thermometer. Place 4 to 6 pieces of chicken into the oil, taking care not to crowd the pan and making sure the pieces don't touch. Cook until the chicken is golden brown and crisp all over and an instant-read thermometer reads 165°F when inserted into the thickest part of a piece, 12 to 15 minutes. As the chicken cooks, use tongs to turn each piece every 2 minutes or so, lowering the heat a little if the chicken begins to darken too quickly and giving the oil enough time to return to 325°F before dropping in the next batch. As each batch is done, remove the chicken to a paper towel–lined plate to absorb excess oil. Repeat until all the chicken is fried. Place the fried chicken on two large platters and serve.

PREP TIME	COOK TIME	SERVES	SmartPoints	CALORIES
20 MINUTES (PLUS OVERNIGHT BRINING)	**12–15** MINUTES	**10**	**21** PER SERVING	**749** PER SERVING

For a girl raised in the South, giving up fried foods wasn't easy at first. This still has the crispiness without the calories.

ART SMITH'S UNFRIED CHICKEN

If you don't want the calories of Art Smith's fried chicken, his unfried chicken is a pretty terrific alternative—super crunchy, so the first bite has that crackle on the outside that you're looking for and the tender, juicy, steaming meat on the inside and, well, see for yourself.

INGREDIENTS:

1 cup buttermilk

1 tablespoon Louisiana hot sauce or hot sauce of choice

2 boneless chicken breasts, cut in half

2 chicken thighs

2 chicken legs

1½ cups multigrain or whole wheat panko breadcrumbs

3 tablespoons grated Parmesan cheese

2 teaspoons freshly ground black pepper

1 teaspoon ground cayenne

1½ teaspoons onion powder

1½ teaspoons garlic powder

1 teaspoon smoked paprika

1 teaspoon salt

Optional: 1 lemon cut into wedges

DIRECTIONS:

In a large bowl, whisk together the buttermilk and hot sauce. Submerge the chicken pieces in the buttermilk mixture, cover, and refrigerate for at least 1 hour but no more than 24 hours.

Preheat the oven to 400°F. In a large zip-top bag, combine the breadcrumbs, Parmesan, black pepper, cayenne, onion powder, garlic powder, smoked paprika, and salt. Seal the bag and shake to combine the ingredients.

Remove the chicken from the buttermilk, let excess drip off, and transfer directly to the bag with the breadcrumb mixture. Shake the bag to evenly coat the chicken in the breadcrumbs. Remove the chicken from the bag and lay flat on a nonstick baking sheet. Place in the oven and bake for 30 minutes, or until cooked through, about 20 minutes. Slice the chicken, arrange onto plates, and serve (with lemon wedges if using).

You can use the same process for anything else you choose to unfry!

PREP TIME	COOK TIME	SERVES	SMARTPOINTS	CALORIES
10 MINUTES (PLUS MARINATING)	30 MINUTES	4	11 PER SERVING	436 PER SERVING

TURKEY LASAGNA

I thought my lasagna-eating days were done, but when I tried this dish for the first time it was *amaaaazeballs*! I took one look at my plate and said, "Where have you been all my life?!" The key is to buy either a really high-quality lean ground turkey product or to buy a boneless, skinless turkey breast and grind it yourself with a few pulses in the food processor.

INGREDIENTS:

Sauce

12 ounces lean ground turkey breast

2 teaspoons granulated garlic

2 teaspoons granulated onion

½ teaspoon ground fennel

3 tablespoons finely chopped fresh flat-leaf parsley

1½ tablespoons finely chopped fresh basil

2 teaspoons salt

¾ teaspoon freshly ground black pepper

2 teaspoons extra virgin olive oil

1 medium onion, finely diced

1½ tablespoons minced fresh garlic

⅓ cup dry white wine

2 (28-ounce) cans whole tomatoes, preferably San Marzano, with juices

Pinch of baking soda (optional)

Lasagna "noodles"

2 large zucchini or summer squash

1 turnip, rutabaga, or celery root, peeled

1 large Japanese eggplant, peeled or unpeeled

1 (8-ounce) package part skim, low-moisture mozzarella cheese, grated

DIRECTIONS:

To make the sauce: Place the turkey in a large bowl. Add the granulated garlic, granulated onion, fennel, parsley, basil, salt, and pepper and, using your hands, mix them all together until seasoning is well incorporated.

In a large saucepan, heat 1 teaspoon of the oil over medium-low heat. Add the onion and cook until softened but not colored, about 5 minutes. Add the garlic and cook for about 1 minute, until aromatic. Scrape the onion and garlic into a bowl. Increase the heat under the pan to medium-high, add the remaining teaspoon oil, then add the seasoned turkey and cook, breaking up the meat with a wooden spoon, for about 10 minutes, until cooked through and lightly browned. Add the wine and cook until absorbed, about 3 minutes. Return the onion and garlic to the pan, then add the tomatoes, crushing them with your hands as they go in. Bring to a simmer, then reduce the heat to medium-low and simmer for 1 hour. Taste and add more salt and/or pepper if needed. If the sauce is a bit acidic, instead of adding sugar, add a pinch of baking soda to balance it out.

To assemble and bake: Preheat the oven to 350°F. Thinly slice the vegetables on a mandoline (page 218) as close to the shape of lasagna noodles as your vegetables allow.

Spread a thin layer of sauce (about one-fifth of the sauce) over the bottom of a lasagna pan. Sprinkle one-fifth of the grated cheese over the sauce. Cover the cheese with half of the zucchini slices. Repeat, making 4 more layers with sauce, cheese, and vegetables, ending with zucchini, then finish the lasagna with the remaining sauce and cheese. Place in the oven and bake for 45 minutes to 1 hour, until the vegetables are tender. Switch the oven to broiler mode. Bring the lasagna pan to the sink and carefully drain excess water from the pan (unlike wheat noodles, vegetable noodles have a high moisture content). Place the lasagna in the broiler and broil until the cheese is lightly browned and bubbly, about 5 minutes. Remove from the oven, cool for 10 minutes, then slice and serve.

PREP TIME	COOK TIME	SERVES	SMARTPOINTS	CALORIES
1 HOUR	1 HOUR	6	5 PER SERVING	261 PER SERVING

GOLDEN CAULIFLOWER COUSCOUS

This dish is pure cauliflower, but we chop it so fine that it has exactly the same texture as couscous. It's actually kind of hard to believe that it's not couscous. There's nothing wrong with couscous— but a cup of it is five points, and a cup of golden cauliflower couscous is only 2 points. I rest my case!

INGREDIENTS:

1 medium head golden cauliflower

1 tablespoon extra virgin olive oil

3 cloves garlic, minced

1 teaspoon ground cumin

1/8 teaspoon ground turmeric

Zest and juice of 1 lemon, or to taste

1 teaspoon fine sea salt, or to taste

1/2 teaspoon freshly ground black pepper, or to taste

1 tablespoon finely chopped red onion

1 Fresno chile, finely chopped

4 black olives, pitted and finely chopped

4 dried apricots, finely chopped

1/2 medium cucumber, peeled, seeded, and finely chopped

1 large tomato, peeled and finely chopped

1 medium orange bell pepper, cored, seeded, and finely chopped

1/4 cup Marcona almonds, chopped

Leaves of 1 small bunch fresh mint, chopped

Leaves of 1 small bunch fresh cilantro, chopped

Leaves of 1 small bunch fresh flat-leaf parsley, chopped

DIRECTIONS:

Remove the core and stems from the cauliflower and separate the florets. In two batches, pulse the cauliflower in a food processor until the granules are the size of couscous, placing each batch in a bowl as it's ready.

Heat the oil in a large nonstick sauté pan over medium heat. Add the garlic and cook for about 1 minute, until aromatic, then stir in the cumin and turmeric and cook, stirring, for about 1 minute, until aromatic. Add the cauliflower and cook, stirring occasionally, for about 5 minutes, until al dente. Transfer the cauliflower to a serving bowl and let cool. Stir in the lemon zest and juice, salt, and pepper, then stir in the onion, chile, olives, apricots, cucumber, tomato, bell pepper, and almonds. Stir in the mint, cilantro, and parsley, taste, and adjust the seasonings with more salt, pepper, and/or lemon juice if needed. Let sit for at least 30 minutes before serving so the flavors can marinate.

PREP TIME	COOK TIME	SERVES	SmartPoints	CALORIES
10 MINUTES	6 MINUTES	6	2 PER SERVING	117 PER SERVING

Cauliflower is a multipurpose vegetable. We roast whole cauliflower, make cauliflower soup, puree cauliflower, and grill large cauliflower "steaks."

TRUFFLE TORTELLONI

Truffle tortelloni might be my favorite food on earth—possibly in the entire solar system! I served these rich little creamy, cheesy, truffled wonders at my Selma Legends Ball, which meant literally thousands had to be made by hand. Everyone grabbed some dough and pitched in, but it was still a two-day project (to serve 400!). Yep, it's a lot of work and a lot of calories, but I promise you'll forget all that the minute you take a bite.

INGREDIENTS:

Truffle pasta dough

1 cup semolina flour, plus more for dusting the pan

½ cup all-purpose flour

¼ cup truffle flour

½ teaspoon Sabatino truffle salt

4 large egg yolks, plus 1 more if needed

½ teaspoon white truffle oil

1 ½ tablespoons cold water

Truffle filling

½ cup mascarpone cheese

½ cup grated (on a Microplane) frozen truffle cheese

½ cup ricotta cheese

½ teaspoon white truffle oil

DIRECTIONS:

Make the dough: In a food processor fitted with a blade attachment, combine the semolina flour, all-purpose flour, truffle flour, and truffle salt. Pulse to combine, then add the egg yolks, truffle oil, and water and run the processor continuously until the dough begins to come together. If the dough is very dry, add 1 additional egg yolk. Turn the dough out onto a work surface and knead until smooth, about 5 minutes, dusting the surface with flour as necessary to prevent sticking. The dough is ready when it forms a smooth, elastic ball and has very few air bubbles when cut. Wrap the dough in plastic wrap and set aside to rest for 30 minutes to 1 hour.

Make the filling: Combine the mascarpone, truffle cheese, ricotta cheese, and truffle oil in a food processor fitted with the blade attachment and process until the mix is smooth and homogenous. Cover and refrigerate the filling until you are ready to use it.

To roll out and fill the pasta: Sprinkle a baking sheet liberally with semolina flour. Secure a pasta roller to a work surface and dust the work surface with flour. Divide the pasta dough into 4 pieces, keeping the pieces you're not working with wrapped in plastic. Dust the dough lightly with flour and,

using your hands, flatten it into a ¼-inch-thick rectangle shape; feel free to add additional flour at any time as you're rolling to keep the dough from sticking.

Set the pasta roller to 1 (the thickest setting) and run the pasta through. Next, set the machine to 2 and run the dough through again. Then set the machine to 3 and work your way progressively through each setting, ending with 6 or 7, depending on how thick you like your pasta. You will have a long, 6-inch-wide strip of pasta dough on your work surface.

Using a pizza wheel or knife, cut the dough lengthwise down the middle to form two 3-inch-long rectangles. Fit a pastry bag with a ½-inch open tip and fill the bag two-thirds full with the filling. Brush the bottom edge of dough lightly with water, then, using the pastry bag, pipe a straight line lengthwise across the dough, leaving enough room to adequately fold the pasta over the filling. You want the line of filling to be about a ½ inch thick. Fold the pasta over the top of the filling, then press the joined edge flat by running a finger firmly along the long edge. Using your

fingers, pinch the pasta into individual pockets of filling, leaving about ¾ inch of sealed pasta between each section.

Using a pastry wheel or knife, cut the sections to separate them, working from the folded filling side toward the sealed flat edge. Place the cut pasta onto a baking sheet sprinkled with semolina flour, keeping the finished pasta covered with plastic wrap as you go. Continue until you run out of filling or dough. At this point, the pasta is ready to be cooked. (Or you can cover with plastic wrap and refrigerate overnight.) To freeze, leave the covered tortelloni on the baking sheet and place in the freezer for 1 hour, then transfer the pasta into freezer bags. The pasta will keep frozen for up to 2 months.

To cook the pasta: Bring a large pot of salted water to a boil. Add the tortelloni, a few at a time, and stir gently to keep them from sticking to the bottom or each other. Keep the heat at a strong simmer and cook for about 5 minutes, until they float to the top of the water. As the tortelloni are done, remove them with a slotted spoon on to plates and serve immediately.

PREP TIME	COOK TIME	SERVES	SMARTPOINTS	CALORIES
2 ½ HOURS	5 MINUTES	6	12 PER SERVING	349 PER SERVING

TRUFFLE TORTELLONI (REDUCED POINTS)

If you've been steering clear of decadent dining for a while, the indulgent version of this pasta might be a little overwhelming, whereas these tortelloni are light little pillows of pleasure—a lot less rich and a lot more healthy, and well worth a try!

INGREDIENTS:

Truffle Tortelloni dough (see page 66)

Filling

2 tablespoons extra virgin olive oil

1 pound wild mushrooms, cleaned, stemmed, and finely chopped

¼ cup minced shallot

2 tablespoons minced garlic

1 tablespoon fresh thyme leaves, chopped

½ teaspoon Sabatino truffle salt

¼ teaspoon freshly ground black pepper

1 cup Chablis wine

2 teaspoons Sabatino Truffle Zest

Sauce

2 cups Great Chicken Stock (page 42)

½ teaspoon xanthan gum

¼ cup grated (on a Microplane) frozen truffle Gouda cheese

1 tablespoon grated (on a Microplane) Parmesan cheese

1 teaspoon white truffle oil

¼ teaspoon Sabatino truffle salt

⅛ teaspoon freshly ground black pepper

Garnishes

Grated Parmesan cheese

Fresh truffle shavings

Thinly sliced fresh chives

You can substitute 2 tablespoons of low-fat crème fraîche for the xanthan gum as a thickening agent if you prefer.

DIRECTIONS:

Make the pasta: Follow the instructions for preparing the Truffle Tortelloni dough on page 66, replacing the mascarpone filling with the mushroom filling.

Make the filling: Heat the oil in a large skillet over medium heat. Add the mushrooms and sauté for 5 minutes, or until they begin to soften. Add the shallots, garlic, and thyme and cook for another 5 minutes, or until the shallots are softened and translucent. Add the truffle salt and pepper, then add the Chablis, increase the heat to high, and cook until nearly all the liquid has cooked off, 5 to 7 minutes. Turn off the heat and stir in the Truffle Zest. Scrape the mushroom filling into a food processor and process until mostly smooth with small chunks of mushrooms still visible. Cool the filling completely.

While the dough is resting, make the sauce: Combine the chicken stock and xanthan gum in a blender and blend briefly, until combined. Pour the stock into a small saucepan, place over medium-high heat, and bring to a boil. Remove from the heat. Whisk in the Gouda cheese, Parmesan cheese, truffle oil, truffle salt, and pepper. The sauce should be light and just coat the back of a spoon. If it doesn't, continue to cook for a little while more to thicken. Reheat just before serving.

To cook the pasta: Bring a large saucepan of water to a boil and salt it. Add the pasta, a few at a time, and stir gently to keep them from sticking to the bottom or each other. Keep the heat at a strong simmer and cook the tortelloni for about 5 minutes, until they float to the top of the water. As the tortelloni are done, remove them with a slotted spoon to bowls. Spoon the hot sauce over the tortelloni and finish with your choice of garnishes.

PREP TIME	COOK TIME	SERVES	SmartPoints	CALORIES
30 MINUTES	**10** MINUTES	**6**	**11** PER SERVING	**356** PER SERVING

For an easy way to decrease points, reduce the amount of cheese and oil you use.

ASPARAGUS PASTA WITH MORELS AND ASPARAGUS MINT PESTO

RECIPE INSPIRED BY CHEF JEAN-GEORGES VONGERICHTEN

Jean-Georges makes this dish and it's spectacular. To cut calories and points, I got inspired to noodle around with the recipe. This version has the same flavors and the same silky quality, minus a lot of the calories. In the summer, sometimes we substitute the pasta noodles with zucchini spaghetti we make using the handy Spiralizer (page 219).

INGREDIENTS:

Pesto

18 medium asparagus spears, woody ends snapped off and discarded

1 cup loosely packed fresh mint leaves

¼ cup extra virgin olive oil

2 tablespoons cold water, or as needed

1 clove garlic, cut in half

1 green Thai chile, stemmed and cut in half

¼ teaspoon salt, or to taste

Pasta

1 ½ cups morel mushrooms

12 jumbo asparagus spears, woody ends snapped off and discarded

1 tablespoon extra virgin olive oil

8 ounces fresh angel-hair pasta

Salt and freshly ground black pepper

8 fresh mint leaves, cut into thin strips

2 ounces Pecorino Romano cheese, grated on a Microplane

Zest of 1 lime

4 lime wedges

You can use 1 cup of spiralized zucchini strips (white part only) to 8 ounces of pasta.

DIRECTIONS:

To make the pesto: Fill a large bowl with water and ice to make an ice-water bath.

Bring a large saucepan of water to a boil. Salt the water, then add the medium asparagus and cook for about 5 minutes, until tender. Remove the asparagus from the water using tongs (do not drain the water), then shock in the ice-water bath until fully cooled. Remove from the ice-water bath and blot dry with paper towels. Chop the asparagus and place it in a blender or food processor. Add the mint, oil, cold water, garlic, chile, and salt and process until smooth, adding more water if the mixture is too thick. Taste and add more salt if needed.

To make the pasta: To clean the morels, fill a bowl with cold water, add the morels, and swish them around in the water. Remove from the water and repeat with two more changes of water. Dry with paper towels and cut the morels in half lengthwise.

Cut the tips off of the asparagus and, using a mandoline or "Y" vegetable peeler, cut the jumbo asparagus into long julienne strips to resemble noodles.

Heat the oil in a large sauté pan over medium-high heat until just smoking. Add the morels and asparagus tips and sauté until softened and lightly browned, about 5 minutes.

Meanwhile, return the asparagus blanching water to a boil, add the pasta, and cook 30 seconds under al dente according to the package directions. Add the asparagus "noodles" and cook for another 30 seconds, until both are al dente. Drain, reserving some of the cooking liquid. Add the pasta and asparagus "noodles" to the pan with the morels, season with salt and pepper, and toss well, adding enough of the reserved cooking liquid to moisten it. Toss in the mint.

Spoon the pesto over the bottom of 4 large bowls and arrange the pasta in the center. Grate some cheese on top and finish with the lime zest. Serve each with a lime wedge.

PREP TIME	COOK TIME	SERVES	SMARTPOINTS	CALORIES
30 MINUTES	10 MINUTES	6	9 PER SERVING	301 PER SERVING

Sweeten the Deal

I usually reserve sweets for holidays and guests, but there are a few treats you'll never catch me turning down. Eating up the three desserts I'm sharing here won't eat up a lot of points. They're simple, old-fashioned, and just perfect with a cup of tea, a pretty plate, and a friend.

FRESH CHERRY CROSTATA

I know people ooh and ahh when a big gooey elaborate dessert is presented. But give me an unpretentious slice of crostata any day! The fresh cherries in this dish capture the essence of summer. This tart is so rustic and homey-looking, it feels like it should show up on **Little House on the Prairie**.

Crust

1 ½ cups all-purpose flour

½ cup cornmeal

1 tablespoon granulated sugar

½ teaspoon salt

¾ cup (1 ½ sticks) cold unsalted butter, cut into ½-inch cubes

½ cup ice-cold water

Filling

3 pounds fresh sweet cherries, pitted

2 tablespoons granulated sugar

2 teaspoons cornstarch

1 tablespoon unsalted butter, melted

2 tablespoons raw sugar

In a medium bowl, whisk together the flour, cornmeal, sugar, and salt. Add the butter and, using your fingers, quickly incorporate it into the dry mixture until it feels like wet sand and has tiny pebbles of butter remaining. Add the water and mix just until the dough begins to come together. Gather up the dough, transfer it to a lightly floured work surface, and knead briefly until it forms a smooth mass. Pat the dough into a ¾-inch-thick disk, wrap in plastic wrap, and refrigerate for at least 1 hour before rolling out. You can make the dough a day ahead.

Preheat the oven to 400°F and line a baking sheet with parchment paper. On a lightly floured surface, roll the dough out to a 15-inch round, then transfer to the prepared baking sheet.

Place the cherries in a large bowl. In a small bowl, whisk together the granulated sugar and cornstarch, then add to the cherries. Mix well with a large spoon or spatula. Arrange the cherries in a mound on top of the dough, leaving a 2-inch rim around the outside. Fold the edge of the dough up and over the fruit.

Brush the melted butter over the pastry crust, then sprinkle with the raw sugar. Place in the oven and bake for 40 minutes, or until the crostata is golden brown on top and bubbly inside. Cool on a wire rack for 10 minutes before slicing and serving.

MAKES 1 (10-INCH) CROSTATA | SERVES 8
13 SMARTPOINTS PER SERVING
418 CALORIES

SPICED APPLESAUCE MINICAKES

When you walk into a house that has something with apples, cinnamon, and cloves baking in the oven, you know you've come home! My grandmother used to make minicakes in a cast-iron skillet, so when Rosie, my chef at the time, started making them, I was just delighted.

1 ½ cups all-purpose flour

2 teaspoons baking soda

1 teaspoon ground cinnamon

1 teaspoon ground ginger

½ teaspoon ground cloves

½ cup wheat bran

1 ¼ cups unsweetened applesauce

¼ cup brown sugar

2 large eggs

¼ cup liquid coconut oil or melted unsalted butter

½ cup golden raisins

You can substitute currants, dried blueberries, or walnuts for the golden raisins.

Preheat the oven to 375°F and line a 12-hole cupcake pan with paper liners.

In a medium bowl, sift together the flour, baking soda, cinnamon, ginger, and cloves. Add the bran and whisk to combine.

In a large bowl, combine the applesauce, brown sugar, eggs, and coconut oil or melted butter and whisk until well blended. Add the dry ingredients to the wet mixture and stir with a rubber spatula or wooden spoon just until it comes together. Add the golden raisins and quickly mix to combine. Spoon the batter into the cupcake liners.

Place in the oven and bake for 20 minutes, or until a tester comes out clean and the tops are just firm to the touch. Remove the pan from the oven and set onto a cooling rack. Serve the minicakes warm or at room temperature with apple butter or jam and a cup of jasmine green tea. The minicakes will keep, wrapped in plastic wrap, at room temperature for up to 3 days or in the freezer for up to 1 month.

SERVES 12

6 SMARTPOINTS PER SERVING

147 CALORIES

LAVENDER SHORTBREAD

Crisp, delicate, and with a heavenly scent. (I love tiny bite-size pieces for myself but nice large pieces if giving as a gift.) We served these lovely cookies to President and Mrs. Obama when they appeared on the show together, and I'm pleased to report that the President, the First Lady, and the shortbread were all a hit!

2 cups all-purpose flour

½ cup white rice flour or cornstarch

3 tablespoons dried lavender flowers, crushed between your palms

1 cup (2 sticks) unsalted butter, at room temperature

2/3 cup sugar, plus more for dusting

1 vanilla bean, split and seeds scraped out

Zest of 1 orange

1 teaspoon salt

Grease a 9½ x 13-inch baking pan. In a large bowl, whisk together the all-purpose flour, rice flour, and lavender flowers and set aside.

In a stand mixer fitted with the paddle attachment or in a large bowl using a hand mixer, cream together the butter, sugar, vanilla seeds, orange zest, and salt until blended, about 1 minute. Turn the mixer to low speed and add the dry mixture a little at a time, beating just until the dough comes together. Using your hands, press the dough in an even layer into the baking pan. Place in the refrigerator for at least 1 hour or up to a day.

Preheat the oven to 350°F. Using a fork, prick the dough across the top (this prevents bubbles from forming). Bake for 15 minutes, remove the pan from the oven, and give the pan a good whack on the counter to get rid of any air pockets. Return the pan to the oven and bake for an additional 15 minutes, or until the shortbread is lightly golden and the center is firm to touch. Remove the pan from the oven, set on a cooling rack, and dust the top evenly with sugar. Cool the shortbread for 10 minutes, then cut into squares. Cool completely before serving. The shortbread will keep wrapped in plastic wrap for up to 1 week or in the freezer for up to 2 months.

MAKES 48 1x2-INCH RECTANGLES

3 SMARTPOINTS PER SERVING

71 CALORIES

Be careful not to over-mix the dough or you'll end up with tough shortbread instead of delicate, flaky goodness.

COLD COMFORT

THE BEST WAY TO CHILL OUT AFTER DINNER

Strawberry Sorbet

The key to a sorbet being any good at all is the quality of the fruit. Buying fruit that has been allowed to ripen on the vine until it is full of flavor is the most important step in any sorbet recipe. If you have great fruit, you will have a great sorbet. Depending on the season and what the dinner or event is, we will vary this recipe in many ways. If we are having Italian food, we might add a little aged balsamic vinegar to the sorbet or ground black pepper, or if we are having Thai food, we'll add minced kaffir lime leaves or lemongrass simple syrup to create an exotic strawberry lime sorbet.

1 quart fresh strawberries, washed and hulled

½ cup superfine sugar

1 teaspoon fresh lemon juice

Pinch of fine sea salt

Combine all the ingredients in a high-speed blender and blend until smooth. Pour into a container and refrigerate until cold, about 2 hours. Pour into an ice cream machine and churn according to the manufacturer's instructions.

MAKES ABOUT **1** QUART | SERVES 8
1 SMARTPOINT PER SERVING
143 CALORIES

Banana Sorbet

How much do I love sorbet? Let me count the ways: It's a refreshing palate cleanser. It runs the gamut from sweet to tangy. It's really, really pretty. Especially if you use the Breville Sorbet Maker (page 218). And though it's got a creamy quality, it has no dairy to make it too rich. We like to get creative with fruits, herbs, even an occasional splash of champagne! But the thing I love most about sorbet is that while it's made with more sugar than ice cream (the sugar comes from fresh fruit), it's got zero fat—and that's cool!

We often serve a similar banana sorbet with toasted walnuts and dark chocolate that has been shaved with a Microplane.

4 cups chopped very ripe bananas
(5 medium bananas)

1 tablespoon banana liqueur

1 tablespoon fresh lemon juice

½ cup light brown sugar

1 teaspoon ground cinnamon

Pinch of ground nutmeg

Seeds of ½ medium vanilla bean

¼ cup water

In a medium nonstick sauté pan, combine the bananas, banana liqueur, lemon juice, brown sugar, cinnamon, and nutmeg. Place over medium heat and bring to a simmer, stirring to dissolve the sugar. Transfer to a blender, add the vanilla bean seeds and water, and blend until smooth. Cool, then place in a container and put in the refrigerator until cold, about 2 hours. Place the mixture in a high-speed blender and blend until smooth. Pour into an ice cream machine and churn according to the manufacturer's instructions.

MAKES ABOUT **3** CUPS | SERVES 6
3 SMARTPOINTS PER SERVING
115 CALORIES

Coconut Lime Sorbet

Lime and coconut sorbet tastes great, but it's higher in points than many sorbets. This one is great when you use a ½ ounce scoop and serve it in a glass with fresh pineapple or your favorite fruit.

1 (15-ounce) can cream of coconut, chilled

1 cup coconut water, chilled

Zest of 2 limes

½ cup fresh lime juice, chilled

Combine all the ingredients in a high-speed blender and blend until smooth. Pour into an ice cream machine and churn according to the manufacturer's instructions.

MAKES ABOUT 3 CUPS | SERVES 12
8 SMARTPOINTS PER SERVING
131 CALORIES

Ginger Peach Sorbet

This refreshing peach sorbet is great with warm roasted or grilled peaches in the summertime.

4 cups chopped ripe peaches (about 6 medium)

½ cup superfine sugar

1 tablespoon pickled ginger

1 tablespoon fresh lemon juice

Pinch of fine sea salt

¼ cup water

Combine all the ingredients in a high-speed blender and blend until smooth. Pour into a container and refrigerate until very cold, about 2 hours. Pour into an ice cream machine and churn according to the manufacturer's instructions.

MAKES ABOUT 1 QUART | SERVES 8
1 SMARTPOINT PER SERVING
77 CALORIES

1 (15-ounce) can lychee fruit, including juices, chilled

¼ cup fresh lime juice, chilled

¾ cup cold water

2 tablespoons vodka

Combine all the ingredients in a high-speed blender and blend until smooth. Pour into an ice cream machine and churn according to the manufacturer's instructions.

Lychee Sorbet

Add a tablespoon of freshly grated ginger to the lychee base for a ginger lychee sorbet. This is great served with a bowl of fresh raspberries.

MAKES ABOUT 3 CUPS | SERVES 6
3 SMARTPOINTS PER SERVING
56 CALORIES

CHAPTER

3

THE FAITH
OF A MUSTARD
SEED

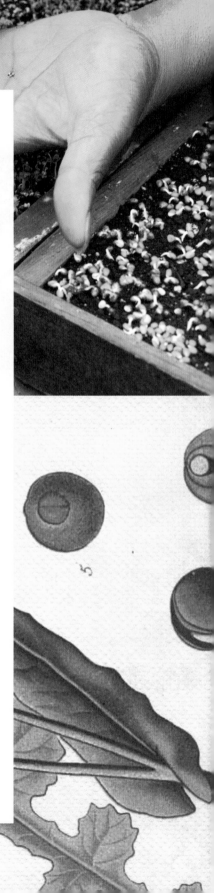

CHAPTER 3
THE FAITH OF A MUSTARD SEED

THERE IS A QUOTE FROM THE BIBLE THAT I'VE ALWAYS CHERISHED: "IF YOUR FAITH IS THE SIZE OF A MUSTARD SEED YOU WILL SAY TO THIS MOUNTAIN, 'MOVE FROM HERE TO THERE,' AND IT WILL MOVE."

Have you ever looked at a mustard seed?
We have them at my farm, and they're *tiny*.
But even at my heaviest, when I sorely doubted
my ability to ever get my eating act together,
I held on to the itty-bittiest grain of faith that
I could shed the weight, or at least move
toward a better way of eating. I found a
better way with Chef Rosie Daley.

The first time I ate a lunch she'd prepared, at a spa I was visiting, I couldn't fathom how such fabulous food amounted to only 300 calories. Each time Rosie cooked, I'd head straight for the spa's kitchen to find out how she'd pulled off yet another low-fat, low-sugar, low-sodium meal that still managed to be utterly delectable. Rosie's food convinced me that "clean eating," as I came to call it, was the way to go. Six months later I convinced her that cooking for me in Chicago was the thing to do! My diet issues were officially solved. Or so I thought.

But it turned out that clean eating was just an excellent first step on a much more complex journey. If I was ever going to really get to a healthy weight—a healthy place—there were more steps I had to take. Literally.

And so it was that I decided to give another spa a try—this time in Colorado. When the fitness director appeared, all I could think was how disappointed he must be to get saddled with me. (I was one of those people who thought you had to be fit to go to the gym.)

I couldn't even bring myself to look him in the eye. If I had, I would have seen a man who was more interested in learning who I was and what had brought me to this juncture than in bullying me into doing push-ups. I would have known that the only one passing judgment on me was me. "It's a pleasure to meet you," the fitness director said. "I'm Bob Greene."

We went for a hike up Bear Creek—or to be more precise: I hiked, Bob coaxed. Somehow we wound our way through two-and-a-half miles of Telluride backwoods, ending at an altitude of about 10,000 feet. Before long, Bob had me lifting weights and using a treadmill. What he didn't have me do was weigh myself. Instead of making my goal a number on the scale, he shifted my focus to a healthier way of being. As we continued our daily excursions, I traded huffing and puffing for walking and talking.

Bob explained why the weight had come back so quickly after my four months of not eating. The fast had slowed my metabolism, and slow metabolism plus no exercise equals weight gain. "That's just science," he

Rosie Daley proved that healthy food could pack a wallop of flavor. And Bob Greene got me moving!

said matter-of-factly. Having such a straightforward explanation somehow eased my guilt.

I believed for a long time that being overweight was some sort of character flaw, but genetics, environment, brain chemistry, and yes, even basic science play a part, too. That's not to say we don't have to take responsibility for our health—of course we do. But Bob made me realize I didn't have to equate being fat with being bad. He helped me see my accomplishments, and in doing so gave me a fresh perspective on what I'd always perceived to be my failings. By the end of our three weeks together, Bob had restored my hope. I left Telluride 12 pounds lighter and feeling much more capable.

Back at work, I still faced the pressures and stress that had always made me reach for the nearest handful of anything I could eat to tamp down my anxiety. But this time when the pounds came back, I reached for the phone instead—and called Bob.

He came. He saw. He asked for a commitment. If he was going to move to Chicago to train me, I had to agree to exercise with him a minimum of 40 minutes every day, regardless of what else was going on in my world—no excuses. I agreed.

Thanks to Rosie, I was already eating low-fat. Now Bob reduced my portion size, added more fruits and vegetables, and got me drinking more water. Walking vigorously with him soon became running; running three miles soon became five miles, which became eight miles, which became a half marathon.

I'd been using my brain and talent and instincts all my life, but I'd never before experienced the thrill of achieving something on the basis of sheer self-discipline. I actually trained, and it actually worked. With each week that passed, I felt leaner, fitter, stronger, and more elated. I was getting healthy in the right way—and I decided to keep up the good work by celebrating my 40th birthday with a full marathon.

Bob warned me that training for a marathon while shooting two shows a day was no small thing. He was not kidding! It often meant waking up at 4:30 in the morning to get my workout in; it always meant running, no matter what. I was ready, willing, and able, until one day when it was raining, and by raining, I mean it was ark-building weather. I explained that I couldn't run in the rain for a very good reason: "It will ruin my hair!" Bob explained that we'd be running anyway, for a very good reason: "YOU'RE GOING!" Perhaps he didn't appreciate the deeply complicated,

Running the Marine Corps Marathon, Washington, D.C.

COMPLETE BEGINNING RUNNER'S SECTION

RUNNER'S

World's Leading Running Magazine

Oprah Did It, So Can You

How She Lost 70 Pounds And Finished The Marathon

America's Top Coaches Share Their Training Secrets

10 Surprising Superfoods

emotionally fraught relationship between a black woman's hair and the rain. How could he? I started to lay out the cultural ramifications: "You don't understand, this is a—" At which point he laid out the logistical implications: "YOU'RE GOING!" We went.

A cold hard rain was also falling the day of the marathon, but thanks to Bob, I was prepared. I wore the number 40 to signify that this would be my rebirth run. I forced myself to drink water. I paced myself with an aim toward nine-minute miles. I paid no mind to the splashes, the puddles, the soaking sneakers, the various landmarks of Washington, D.C., where the race was taking place, or the 15,000 other runners; the cheering crowds had begun to blur. I kept my head in the game, just as Bob and I had strategized. By the 21st mile my calves were concrete. By the 22nd mile my knees were throbbing. By mile 23 my thighs were jelly. By mile 24 I couldn't distinguish the aches from the pains. At the 26th mile, my entire body was threatening to implode. Still, I kept going. I was running in the rain for every morning I'd ever woken up hating the way I felt, for every night I'd ever gone to bed praying I could find a new way forward. I was running for every

confrontation I'd ever avoided, every feeling I'd ever repressed, and every birthday wish that hadn't come true. I was running for my life.

I've seen some truly gorgeous things in my life: Mississippi fireflies lighting up the sky just beyond my grandmother's front porch. The girls from my South African leadership academy making strides in their young lives. The sun rising over Haleakala National Park on Maui. The incomparably majestic Grand Canyon. But after four hours and 29 minutes of pushing my body to do what only a mustard-seed-size part of me believed it could, that finish line was quite possibly the most miraculous sight I'd ever beheld. Literally, a sight for sore eyes.

Of course, faith alone didn't get me across the finish line. It was faith strengthened by the fuel of healthy food. When my body started trusting that I'd give it what it needed, it was able to start giving back to me. That was a life-changing lesson. And so was this: I didn't have to sacrifice to eat well. Rosie and all the amazing chefs who followed her taught me that healthy eating needn't be dreary or monotonous. But don't just take my word for it—the enticing recipes that follow prove it!

Bob helped me think less about my size and more about my health. We've been working together ever since!

The Oprah Winfrey Leadership Academy for Girls began as a conversation in Nelson Mandela's living room, and I believe it will end with a better world!

The key to great roast chicken is to pat the skin dry very thoroughly after rinsing off the brine, otherwise the skin won't get nice and crispy.

BRINED AND ROASTED CHICKEN

Brining not only adds flavor and juiciness, it makes chicken fall-off-the-bone tender. A brine is normally a sugar, salt, and spice mixture added to water. For Weight Watchers, I normally remove the sugar or substitute it with a touch of agave syrup. I brine a 3.5 pound chicken for 12 hours, though you can do it for less.

INGREDIENTS:

2 fresh thyme sprigs

2 fresh rosemary sprigs

2 quarts water

1 rib celery, chopped

1 small carrot, chopped

1 small yellow onion, chopped

½ cup peeled and smashed garlic cloves

1½ teaspoons whole black peppercorns

1 bay leaf

⅓ cup fine sea salt

1 (3½-pound) chicken, neck and giblets removed

1 teaspoon extra virgin olive oil

DIRECTIONS:

Tie the thyme and rosemary together with kitchen twine to make an herb bundle.

In a large nonreactive pot, combine 1 quart of the water, the celery, carrot, onion, garlic, peppercorns, bay leaf, herb bundle, and salt, place over high heat, and bring to a boil, stirring to dissolve the salt. Immediately remove from the heat, add the remaining 1 quart water, and cool completely. Pour the brine into a nonreactive container large enough to hold the chicken. Add the chicken to the brine, submerging it completely. Place in the refrigerator to brine for at least 4 hours or up to overnight.

Preheat the oven to 450°F. Remove the chicken from the brine, discard the brine, and pat dry with paper towels. Place the chicken on a roasting pan fitted with a roasting rack and rub the oil over the chicken. Place the pan in the middle rack of the oven with the legs facing back. Roast the chicken for 1 hour to 1 hour and 15 minutes, turning the chicken halfway through, until an instant-read thermometer inserted into the deepest part of a thigh registers 160°F. Remove the chicken from the oven, let rest for about 20 minutes, then carve and serve.

PREP TIME	COOK TIME	SERVES	SMARTPOINTS	CALORIES
8–10 HOURS (INCLUDING OVERNIGHT BRINING)	1 HOUR	4	5 PER SERVING	297 PER SERVING

SUSTAINABLE HALIBUT À LA GRECQUE

RECIPE INSPIRED BY CHEF LAWRENCE McFADDEN

Look for Greenland turbot halibut caught in Alaska for the most sustainable option.
For a slightly more budget-friendly variation, this recipe also works
with black bass or cod.

INGREDIENTS:

"À la Grecque" cooking liquid

½ cup champagne vinegar

1 cup Great Chicken Stock (page 42)

1 cup Chablis

2 bay leaves

6 sprigs fresh thyme

1 ½ teaspoons coriander seeds, toasted

¼ cup very thinly sliced shallots

Fish and vegetables

Extra virgin olive oil cooking spray

12 medium cremini mushrooms, quartered

6 French breakfast radishes

1 tablespoon fresh lemon juice

6 baby artichokes

6 (6-ounce, 1-inch-thick) halibut fillets

Salt and freshly ground black pepper

1 cup fresh English peas

2 medium tomatoes, peeled, seeded, and finely chopped

12 fresh basil leaves, torn into pieces

Leftover halibut makes for great fish tacos! →

DIRECTIONS:

Combine all of the cooking liquid ingredients in a container, cover, and marinate in the refrigerator for at least 2 hours or up to 24 hours.

Preheat the oven to 400°F. Coat a baking sheet with cooking spray. Place the quartered mushrooms and radishes on the sheet and spray them with cooking spray. Roast for 10 to 15 minutes, until they are lightly browned and softened.

Pour 4 cups of water into a large bowl and add the lemon juice. To prepare the baby artichokes, remove the outer leaves, trim the stems, and trim the outside green layer of the artichoke base. Cut each artichoke in half lengthwise, remove the choke using a paring knife, and discard it. Discard the top section of the leaves. Cut each half of the artichoke lengthwise into thirds and submerge the artichokes in the lemon water.

In a large saucepan, bring the cooking liquid to a boil over high heat, then turn off the heat. Season the halibut with salt and pepper. Heat a large skillet, preferably cast-iron, and coat it with cooking spray. Place the fish in the skillet and cook without moving it until nicely browned on the bottom, 3 to 5 minutes. Using a fish spatula, transfer the fish to a baking dish just large enough to fit the fish in one layer with the browned side up. Strain the cooking liquid, discarding the solids, and pour the cooking liquid around (not directly over) the fish, taking care not to cover the top of the fish with liquid. Place the fish in the oven and bake until it is opaque throughout and flakes easily, about 15 minutes.

While the fish is in the oven, remove the baby artichokes from the water, pat them dry with paper towels, and season with salt. Heat a large skillet over medium heat and coat with cooking spray. Add the baby artichokes and cook until they start to soften, 5 to 7 minutes. Add the mushrooms, radishes, peas, and tomatoes and cook until the artichokes are tender and all ingredients are heated through, adding a few drops of water if the mixture begins to brown or stick to the pan.

Divide the fish among individual shallow bowls. To each, add about ⅓ cup of the cooking liquid and an equal amount of the vegetables. Finish each dish with some basil and serve.

PREP TIME	COOK TIME	SERVES	SMARTPOINTS	CALORIES
30	**30**	**6**	**4**	**246**
MINUTES	MINUTES		PER SERVING	PER SERVING
(PLUS OVERNIGHT MARINATING)				

FARRO WITH PEAS, ASPARAGUS, PEA PESTO, AND CURED OLIVES

The sweetness of the peas, the saltiness of the olives, the woodsiness of the asparagus, and the creamy herbal pesto against the texture of the grain make this one of my favorite recipes.

INGREDIENTS:

Salt

¾ cup pearled farro (or substitute spelt, wheat berries, or barley)

6 stalks asparagus, woody ends snapped off

1 cup fresh shelled peas or thawed frozen petite peas

½ cup oil-cured olives, pitted and cut in half

½ cup Pea Pesto (recipe on facing page)

2 cups arugula

¼ cup thinly sliced fresh chives

Freshly ground black pepper

¼ cup grated (on a Microplane) Parmesan cheese

¼ cup pine nuts, toasted

DIRECTIONS:

Bring a large pot of well-salted water to a boil. Add the farro and cook until al dente, 20 to 25 minutes. Drain, rinse with cold water, and place in a serving bowl.

Meanwhile, fill a large bowl with ice and water to make an ice-water bath. Fill a second large saucepan with water and bring to a boil over high heat. Salt the water, then add the asparagus and boil until al dente, about 3 minutes, a little more or less depending on how thick the stalks are. Using a slotted spoon, remove the asparagus from the pan and transfer to the ice-water bath to cool. Remove the asparagus from the ice-water bath, pat dry with paper towels, then thinly slice the asparagus on the diagonal. Add the peas to the simmering water and cook until al dente, about 1 minute. Drain, transfer to the ice-water bath, then drain again and pat dry with paper towels.

Add the asparagus, peas, and olives to the farro, then add the pesto and stir to coat the ingredients in the pesto. Toss in the arugula and chives. Season with salt and pepper, top with the Parmesan and pine nuts, and serve.

PREP TIME	COOK TIME	SERVES	SmartPoints	CALORIES
25 MINUTES	30 MINUTES	6	9 PER SERVING	294 PER SERVING

If you're a fan of quinoa, you'll love farro, one of my favorite grains!

PEA PESTO

MAKES ABOUT 2 CUPS | 4 SmartPoints per ¼ cup

1 cup fresh shelled or thawed frozen peas

3 tablespoons extra virgin olive oil

2 cups loosely packed fresh basil leaves

3 cloves garlic

2 ounces Parmesan cheese, chopped

¼ cup walnut halves, toasted

Juice of 2 lemons

Zest of 2 lemons

½ teaspoon sea salt, or to taste

Fill a large bowl with ice and water to make an ice-water bath. Fill a small saucepan with water and bring to a boil over high heat. Salt the water, then add the peas and cook until al dente, about 1 minute. Drain, transfer to the ice-water bath, then drain again and pat dry with paper towels. (To save time and a pot to wash, blanch the peas as you blanch the vegetables for the salad above.)

In a food processor, combine the peas, oil, basil, garlic, Parmesan, walnuts, and lemon juice and blend to a rough puree. Add the lemon zest and salt and pulse to combine. The pesto will keep covered in the refrigerator for up to 1 week.

TEA-SMOKED WILD SALMON

If you've never tea-smoked your salmon, the time has come! The flavor all depends on your choice of tea leaves. I've tried everything from gunpowder tea to Lapsang souchong, and I find tea with a smoky flavor works best. I prefer to keep my salmon in one piece for this recipe, but you can easily use fillets. This recipe pairs well with the Spring Pea Soup (page 35) or the Grilled Asparagus (page 216).

INGREDIENTS:

Marinade

⅓ cup soy sauce

1 tablespoon agave nectar

Zest and juice of ½ orange

1 clove garlic, grated on a Microplane

1 teaspoon minced or grated (on a Microplane) ginger

Zest of 1 lime

Juice of 2 limes

½ teaspoon red pepper flakes

1 ½ pounds king salmon, skin removed

For smoking the salmon

(NOTE: THESE INGREDIENTS ARE NOT EATEN)

¼ cup uncooked jasmine rice

¼ cup jasmine or black tea leaves

3 tablespoons brown sugar

6 whole star anise

1 thumb-size piece fresh ginger, sliced

6 black peppercorns

1 cinnamon stick, crushed

Extra virgin olive oil cooking spray

Garnishes

1 teaspoon toasted sesame oil

½ cup thinly sliced scallions, white and green parts

½ cup chopped fresh cilantro leaves

1 tablespoon black sesame seeds

DIRECTIONS:

To make the marinade: In a small bowl, whisk together all the marinade ingredients. Place the salmon in a large zip-top bag and pour the marinade over the fish. Secure the bag, place it in a bowl and place in the refrigerator to marinate for 1 to 2 hours, turning the bag occasionally to make sure all parts of the salmon soak in the marinade. Remove the salmon from the marinade and discard the marinade and bag. Place the salmon on a plate and pat dry with paper towels. Put it back in the refrigerator for at least 1 hour or up to overnight. When you take it out, it should feel dry but slightly sticky—this will allow the fish to soak up as much of the smoke flavor as possible. Now get ready to smoke!

To smoke the salmon: Line a wok or stovetop smoker with 2 squares of heavy-duty foil. In a small bowl, combine the rice, tea leaves, brown sugar, star anise, ginger, peppercorns, and cinnamon and spread the mixture on top of the foil. Fold the edges of the foil over the mixture to make a packet. Heat over medium-high heat until it starts to smoke. Put a wire rack or metal vegetable steamer over the smoking spices and place the salmon on top. Lightly coat with cooking spray and cover the wok with a lid. Reduce the heat to low and smoke for 20 minutes, or until the salmon is a beautiful mahogany color and just cooked through. Cooking time will vary depending on the thickness of the fish. Serve drizzled with the sesame oil and scattered with the scallions, cilantro, and black sesame seeds.

PREP TIME	COOK TIME	SERVES	SMARTPOINTS	CALORIES
4 HOURS (INCLUDING 2 HRS FOR MARINADE)	30 MINUTES	4	9 PER SERVING	346 PER SERVING

KABOCHA SQUASH COMPOTE

Not only is kabocha squash a great source of iron, vitamin C, and beta-carotene,
but a cup contains 40 calories and half the carbs of butternut squash.

INGREDIENTS:

DIRECTIONS:

Think of it as a collection of winter vegetables' greatest hits.

Compote

¼ cup chopped pecans

1 cup cubed (½-inch cubes) rutabaga

1 cup cubed (½-inch cubes) parsnip

1 cup cubed (½-inch cubes) kabocha squash

1 ½ tablespoons extra virgin olive oil

1 teaspoon grated (on a Microplane) garlic

1 teaspoon peeled and grated (on a Microplane) ginger

½ teaspoon ground fennel

½ teaspoon ground cumin

¼ teaspoon ground turmeric

¼ teaspoon ground cayenne

½ teaspoon salt

Dressing

1 tablespoon Dijon-style mustard

2 tablespoons apple cider vinegar

1 teaspoon grated (on a Microplane) garlic

1 teaspoon peeled and grated (on a Microplane) ginger

¼ cup extra virgin olive oil

½ teaspoon salt

¼ teaspoon freshly ground black pepper

Salad

¼ green or red apple

1 tablespoon fresh lemon juice

1 bunch baby arugula

1 baby gem lettuce

2 tablespoons dried cranberries, soaked in water
to cover for 30 minutes and drained

¼ cup shaved (with a vegetable peeler) Parmesan cheese

To make the compote: Preheat the oven to 350°F. Place the pecans on a small baking sheet or ovenproof skillet and toast, stirring a couple of times, until browned and fragrant, 7 to 10 minutes. Remove from the oven and transfer to a plate to cool.

Meanwhile, combine the rutabaga, parsnip, and squash in a large bowl. Add the oil, garlic, ginger, fennel, cumin, turmeric, cayenne, and salt and toss to coat. Place in a small baking pan (a pie plate works nicely), cover with foil, and roast for 15 minutes. Remove the foil and roast for an additional 15 to 20 minutes, until tender.

To make the dressing: In a small bowl, whisk the mustard, vinegar, garlic, and ginger. Whisk in the oil until emulsified, then add the salt and pepper.

To make the salad: Dice the apple and toss it with the lemon juice. Combine the arugula, baby gem lettuce, and apple in a salad bowl. Toss with half of the dressing, or more if needed to coat the leaves lightly, and place on the center of each of 6 plates. Surround the greens with the pecans, roasted vegetables, and cranberries and serve topped with the Parmesan.

PREP TIME	COOK TIME	SERVES	SmartPoints	CALORIES
20 MINUTES	**30** MINUTES	**6**	**7** PER SERVING	**237** PER SERVING

MISO-GLAZED COD

Based on the classic Nobu recipe, this quick midweek meal is sweet, savory, decadent, and low in points!
I love to pair it with spicy, sesame-scented green beans and, my favorite, forbidden black rice with
chives. Miso, which is made mostly from fermented soybeans, is a nutritional superstar.

One of my favorite fish dishes for company!

INGREDIENTS:

Fish

6 tablespoons mirin

2 tablespoons sake

6 tablespoons white miso paste

3 tablespoons agave nectar

Zest of 1 lime

1 teaspoon grated fresh ginger

1 small clove garlic, grated

6 cod fillets, skin and bones removed

1 teaspoon salt

Grapeseed oil spray

Freshly chopped fresh chives and cilantro

Sesame Green Beans

12 ounces fresh haricots verts or green beans,
ends trimmed

1 teaspoon toasted sesame oil

1 teaspoon black sesame seeds

½ teaspoon red pepper flakes

DIRECTIONS:

In a small bowl, whisk together the mirin, sake, miso
paste, agave, lime zest, ginger, and garlic. Place the
fish in a large zip-top bag, add the marinade, secure
the bag, and refrigerate overnight.

When you are ready to prepare dinner, turn the
broiler to high.

Fill a medium saucepan with 1 quart water and add
1 teaspoon salt. Place over high heat and bring to a boil.

While the water is coming up to a boil, remove the
fish from the marinade and place it in a broiler-
proof dish in one layer. Lightly wipe off any excess
marinade, but do not rinse the fish. Spray the fish
lightly with oil and broil for 8 to 10 minutes, until
the fish is opaque and the surface of the fish has a
caramelized look to it.

While the fish is in the broiler, add the green beans
to the boiling water and cook for 3 minutes, or until
al dente. Drain the green beans, place them in a bowl,
and toss with the toasted sesame oil, black sesame
seeds, and red pepper flakes.

Divide the fish and green beans among plates and
garnish with the chives and cilantro.

PREP TIME	COOK TIME	SERVES	SmartPoints	CALORIES
15 MINUTES (PLUS MARINATING TIME)	**7** MINUTES	**6**	**7** PER SERVING	**273** PER SERVING

POTATO-CRUSTED SUSTAINABLE CHILEAN SEA BASS

The problem with cooking most fish is that it can go really wrong, really fast. Grab a quick phone call and three minutes later you've got a dried-out mess. But sustainable Chilean sea bass is extremely forgiving. If someone is running late, I just turn down the heat!

INGREDIENTS:

4 (6-ounce, 1-inch-thick) pieces sea bass, in rectangular shapes

2 large russet potatoes, peeled

Extra virgin olive oil cooking spray

Sea salt

1 tablespoon grapeseed oil

1 medium lemon, cut into quarters

The potato crust gives the dish a yummy crunchy exterior.

DIRECTIONS:

Rinse the sea bass and pat dry with paper towels. Set the fish onto a plate, cover with plastic wrap, and refrigerate while you prepare the potato.

Using a mandoline, cut long, paper-thin slices of potatoes. Place the potato strips in a large bowl, coat with cooking spray, and season lightly with salt.

Place the potato strips onto a piece of plastic wrap in this manner: First, set down 2 potato strips overlapping lengthwise by 1 inch to make one 6- to 8-inch-long strip. Lay down 2 more strips next to the first, overlapping by ½ inch. Repeat to make 4 or 5 rows of overlapping slices, enough to fully cover the fish. Place the fish at the end of the potato strip closest to you. Lift the plastic wrap and roll the fish in the potato until it is completely wrapped and the bottom of the fish has about a ¾-inch overlap. Wrap the fish tightly in the plastic wrap. Repeat with the remaining potatoes and fish and refrigerate the fish for 15 minutes.

Heat the oil in a large nonstick sauté pan over medium heat. Unwrap the fish from the plastic wrap and carefully place the fish in the pan seam side down. Cook until the potatoes on the bottom are golden brown, about 4 minutes, adjusting the heat up or down as needed to evenly brown the potatoes. Carefully turn the fish over and cook for about 4 minutes, until the potatoes are golden brown on the second side and the fish is flaky inside. Divide among plates, garnish each with a lemon quarter, and serve.

PREP TIME	COOK TIME	SERVES	SmartPoints	CALORIES
20 MINUTES	10 MINUTES	4	7 PER SERVING	302 PER SERVING

SUSTAINABLE CHILEAN SEA BASS WITH LEMON FENNEL CHUTNEY

This versatile fish is a buttery, melt-in-your-mouth fillet that's substantial enough to be filling. All you need is a good sauvignon blanc and someone to share it with!

INGREDIENTS:

Chutney

Extra virgin olive oil cooking spray

1 medium yellow onion, diced

1 medium bulb fennel, top trimmed, cored, and diced

¼ teaspoon kosher salt

1 cup water

2 teaspoons honey

1 teaspoon ground coriander

3 cloves garlic, peeled

Zest and juice of 1 lemon

¼ cup golden raisins, chopped

½ teaspoon yellow mustard seeds

1 tablespoon rice vinegar

1 tablespoon champagne vinegar

¼ cup Pernod

¼ teaspoon freshly ground black pepper

16 fresh cilantro leaves, roughly chopped

Sea Bass

8 (6-ounce, 1-inch-thick) pieces Chilean sea bass

1 teaspoon fine sea salt

¼ teaspoon granulated garlic

½ teaspoon freshly ground white pepper

Extra virgin olive oil cooking spray

Lemon wedges (optional)

DIRECTIONS:

Make the chutney: Coat a medium skillet with cooking spray and heat over medium-low heat. Add half of the diced onion, the fennel, and salt and cook, stirring occasionally, until translucent, about 5 minutes.

While the fennel mixture is cooking, combine the remaining onion, the water, honey, coriander, garlic, lemon zest and juice, the raisins, mustard seeds, rice vinegar, and champagne vinegar in a blender, preferably a high-speed one, and blend until smooth.

Pour the Pernod into the pan with the cooked onion and fennel and cook until evaporated, then add the mixture from the blender. Increase the heat to high and cook until the chutney has thickened, about 3 minutes, then remove it from the heat. Add the black pepper and cool to room temperature. Stir in the cilantro.

Make the sea bass: Season the fish on both sides with the salt, granulated garlic, and white pepper. Coat a cast-iron skillet with cooking spray and heat over medium-high heat. Place the fish in the skillet and cook for 4 minutes, or until the bottom is golden brown. Using a wide spatula, carefully turn the fish over and cook for 3 to 4 minutes more, until it becomes opaque throughout and flakes easily. Divide the fish among plates and serve with a tablespoon of the chutney and a squeeze of lemon if you like.

PREP TIME	COOK TIME	SERVES	SMARTPOINTS	CALORIES
15	30	8	3	176
MINUTES	MINUTES		PER SERVING	PER SERVING

It's like the navy blue blazer of seafood.

CHAKALAKA

When the girls from my South African leadership academy are visiting—which is quite often—they ask for chakalaka. Once I figured out what it actually was, it became a regular part of my repertoire! Sometimes a little familiar food is a terrific way to stave off homesickness.

INGREDIENTS:

1 tablespoon extra virgin olive oil

1 medium yellow onion, finely diced

3 cloves garlic, minced

½ teaspoon minced fresh ginger

2 teaspoons Madras curry powder

1 teaspoon ground cayenne

½ teaspoon dried thyme

¼ teaspoon smoked paprika

2 medium plum tomatoes, peeled, seeded, and diced

4 cups thinly sliced cabbage

2 jalapeño chiles, seeded and diced

1 large carrot, grated

1 medium red bell pepper, cored, seeded, and diced

1 ½ cups cooked white beans

2 tablespoons distilled white vinegar

1 teaspoon fine sea salt

½ teaspoon freshly ground black pepper

2 tablespoons chopped fresh flat-leaf parsley

DIRECTIONS:

Heat the oil in a large saucepan over medium heat. Add the onion and cook for 2 minutes, or until softened. Add the garlic and ginger and cook for 1 minute, or until aromatic. Add the curry powder, cayenne, thyme, and smoked paprika and cook for about 1 minute, until aromatic, adding a tiny bit of water if the mixture starts to stick to the bottom of the pan. Add the tomatoes, cabbage, chiles, carrot, and bell pepper, bring to a simmer, and simmer for about 5 minutes, stirring occasionally, until the vegetables begin to soften. Add the beans and vinegar and cook for an additional 2 to 3 minutes, until the beans are warmed through. Add the salt and pepper and stir in the parsley. Serve hot or warm, or refrigerate and serve cold.

PREP TIME	COOK TIME	SERVES	SmartPoints	CALORIES
15 MINUTES	15 MINUTES	6	3 PER SERVING	137 PER SERVING

This is an awesome accompaniment to fish, grilled meats, or poultry.

MONKFISH WITH CITRUS LENTILS

The good news about monkfish is that a three-ounce serving comes to 82 calories and zero carbs. And the even better news about lentils is that they're magic! Lentils help protect the heart and digestive system, they aid in stabilizing blood sugar, controlling cholesterol, and keeping your appetite in check. This recipe is what I call a win-win combination.

INGREDIENTS:

Citrus Lentils

2 quarts water

2 cups French green lentils

Sea salt

Extra virgin olive oil cooking spray

1 medium shallot, finely diced

1 teaspoon paprika

1 teaspoon red pepper flakes

2 teaspoons fresh thyme leaves, chopped

3 cloves garlic, minced

2 teaspoons tomato paste

3 cups Great Chicken Stock (page 42), plus more if needed

Zest and juice of 1 medium orange

Zest and juice of 1 medium lime

1 bay leaf

Freshly ground black pepper

Fish

6 (6-ounce) monkfish loins, bones removed

Salt and freshly ground black pepper

Extra virgin olive oil cooking spray

1 lemon

DIRECTIONS:

To make the lentils: Pour 2 quarts water into a large saucepan and add the lentils and 1 tablespoon salt. Place over high heat and bring to a boil. Immediately drain and rinse under cold running water. Set aside.

Rinse the pan out, dry it, and coat it with cooking spray. Heat over medium-low heat, add the shallot, and cook until translucent, about 3 minutes. Add the paprika, red pepper flakes, thyme, and garlic and cook for about 1 minute, until fragrant, adding a tiny bit of water if the mixture starts to stick. Add the tomato paste and cook, stirring, for 2 minutes, again adding a tiny bit of water if the mixture starts to stick. Add the lentils, chicken stock, orange juice, lime juice, and bay leaf. Increase the heat to medium-high, bring to a simmer, then reduce the heat to low and simmer for 15 to 25 minutes, until the lentils are tender but not mushy. Remove the bay leaf. Transfer a quarter of the mixture to a blender and blend until smooth. Fold the pureed lentils back into the pan. Add the citrus zest and season with salt and pepper.

To make the fish: Season the fish with salt and pepper. Heat a large skillet, preferably cast-iron, over medium-high heat and spray with cooking spray. Add the fish and cook for about 3 minutes per side, until it is lightly browned and cooked through.

To serve: Divide the lentils among plates and add the fish to the plates. Squeeze a little lemon juice over the fish and serve.

PREP TIME	COOK TIME	SERVES	SMARTPOINTS	CALORIES
15 MINUTES	30 MINUTES	6	9 PER SERVING	416 PER SERVING

I used to do this dish with ham hocks, but the smoked turkey is a much healthier substitute.

FAVA BEAN AND SMOKED TURKEY SALAD

If the only thing you know about fava beans is that Hannibal Lecter paired them with "a nice Chianti," try this dish! We have it just a few times a year, because though we grow fava beans on the farm in Santa Barbara, California, the season is very short—they peak in spring.

INGREDIENTS:

Jalapeño Basil Vinaigrette

3 tablespoons extra virgin olive oil

2 tablespoons distilled white vinegar

Zest and juice of 1 medium lemon

½ medium jalapeño chile, seeded and chopped

1 teaspoon Dijon-style mustard

½ teaspoon freshly ground black pepper

½ teaspoon fine sea salt

¼ cup fresh basil leaves cut into ribbons

Salad

Salt

1 cup fresh fava beans, shelled

Extra virgin olive oil cooking spray

1 medium Yukon gold potato, peeled and diced

1 cup diced skinless smoked turkey thigh

2 tablespoons fresh mint cut into thin ribbons

2 tablespoons chopped fresh flat-leaf parsley

½ teaspoon red pepper flakes

1 cup chopped (½-inch pieces) baby gem lettuce

¼ cup thinly shaved Parmesan cheese

DIRECTIONS:

To make the vinaigrette: Combine all of the ingredients except the basil in a blender and blend until smooth. Pour the dressing into a medium bowl and fold in the basil.

To make the salad: Fill a medium bowl with ice and water to create an ice-water bath. Fill a medium saucepan with water, place over high heat, and bring to a boil. Salt the water, then add the fava beans and blanch them for 1 minute. Drain and immediately plunge them into the ice-water bath to cool. Drain, peel the fava beans, then place them in the dressing to marinate.

Coat a nonstick skillet with cooking spray and heat over medium-high heat. Add the diced potatoes and cook until golden brown on the outside and cooked through, about 5 minutes. Add the smoked turkey and cook to warm through, then transfer to a serving bowl to cool to room temperature. Add the mint, parsley, and red pepper flakes. Add the fava beans with their vinaigrette and toss to combine, then add the lettuce and toss lightly to combine. Divide the salad among plates, garnish with the Parmesan, and serve.

PREP TIME	COOK TIME	SERVES	SMARTPOINTS	CALORIES
15 MINUTES	10 MINUTES	4	7 PER SERVING	273 PER SERVING

"IF YOU DO WORK THAT YOU LOVE, AND THE WORK FULFILLS YOU, THE REST WILL COME."

— OPRAH WINFREY

Morning Glories

Recipe lovingly provided by Imelda Chavez

IME'S GLUTEN-FREE COCONUT BANANA MUFFINS

2 cups almond flour

½ cup unsweetened shredded coconut

1 ½ teaspoons baking powder

½ teaspoon baking soda

1 tablespoon ground cinnamon

¾ teaspoon salt

4 medium very ripe bananas

3 large eggs

3 tablespoons unsalted butter, melted and cooled

1 ½ tablespoons honey

1 tablespoon apple cider vinegar

1 teaspoon grated (on a Microplane) lemon zest

¼ cup chopped pecans

¾ cup coarsely shredded carrots

6 dried apricots, finely chopped

Preheat the oven to 325°F and line a 12-cup muffin pan with paper liners.

In a large bowl, whisk together the almond flour, coconut, baking powder, baking soda, cinnamon, and salt.

Coarsely mash the bananas in a medium bowl. In a separate bowl, beat the eggs, then whisk in the butter, honey, vinegar, and lemon zest. Stir in the mashed bananas. Lightly fold the wet ingredients into dry ingredients until just combined (do not overmix). Fold in the pecans, carrots, and apricots.

Divide the batter among the muffin cups, filling them three-quarters full. Place in the oven and bake for 35 to 45 minutes, until golden brown on top and a toothpick inserted in the center of a muffin comes out clean. Place the pan on a cooling rack to cool for about 5 minutes, then remove the muffins from the pan and serve.

MAKES 12 MUFFINS

7 SMARTPOINTS PER MUFFIN | 240 CALORIES

I used to skip breakfast, thinking I was saving calories. Now it's the one meal I for sure won't miss. Whether it's "The Usual" (page 110), which I have some version of on most days, or just a breakfast cookie and a chai on the run, breakfast sets the tone (not to mention the blood sugar) for the rest of my day. If I eat well in the morning I'm often not hungry until late afternoon.

BANANA WALNUT OATMEAL

4 cups water

1 cup steel-cut oats, such as McCann's Irish Steel Cut Oatmeal

1 banana, sliced

½ cup toasted walnuts

Garnishes

Sprinkle of cinnamon

Swirl of raw honey

Pat of butter

Splash of almond milk

Fresh blueberries

Bring the water to a boil in a medium saucepan. Add the oats, return to a boil, then reduce the heat to low and simmer for about 20 minutes, stirring occasionally and scraping the bottom of the pan, until thick and creamy. Add the banana and cook for an additional 5 minutes. Spoon into bowls, top with the walnuts and your choice of garnishes, and serve.

SERVES 4

8 SMARTPOINTS PER SERVING | 281 CALORIES

POTATO HASH

4 medium unpeeled Yukon gold potatoes, cut into ½-inch cubes

Extra virgin olive oil cooking spray

1 link andouille chicken sausage, diced

1 small red onion, diced

1 medium red bell pepper, cored, seeded, and diced

1 medium jalapeño chile, minced

2 medium scallions, white and green parts, sliced ¼ inch thick

Fine sea salt

1 tablespoon blackening seasoning

1 tablespoon apple cider vinegar

2 tablespoons finely chopped fresh chives

1 tablespoon finely chopped fresh rosemary

Freshly ground black pepper

Place the potatoes into a colander, rinse them under cold water, dry them with a kitchen towel, and set aside.

Coat a large cast-iron skillet with cooking spray and set the pan over high heat to get it very hot. Add the sausage and cook, stirring often with a metal spatula, until it browns and starts to caramelize, about 5 minutes. Scrape the sausage from the pan into a medium bowl and set it aside.

Add the onion, bell pepper, chile, and scallions to the pan you cooked the sausage in, season with salt, and cook over medium heat until the vegetables just begin to soften, about 3 minutes. Remove the vegetables from the pan and add them to the sausage.

Again return the same pan to the stovetop, add the potatoes, and cook over medium heat until they are about three-quarters cooked, about 10 minutes, then add the sausage, vegetables, and blackening seasoning and cook until the potatoes are cooked through and crisp, another 3 to 4 minutes. Stir in the vinegar, chives, and rosemary and season with black pepper. Taste and add more salt and/or pepper if needed.

SERVES 4

6 SMARTPOINTS PER SERVING | 229 CALORIES

BREAKFAST COOKIES

1 ½ cups rolled oats

Cooking spray

2 small Gala apples, peeled, cored, and roughly chopped

4 medium ripe bananas, mashed

⅓ cup apple juice

1 ¼ cups walnuts, roughly chopped

¾ cup dried apples, minced

½ cup raisins

½ cup plus 1 tablespoon oat flour

1 ½ teaspoons ground ginger

1 teaspoon ground cinnamon

½ teaspoon ground cloves

½ teaspoon ground mace

½ teaspoon ground nutmeg

½ teaspoon baking powder

½ teaspoon salt

Preheat the oven to 350° and line a baking sheet with a silicone baking mat or parchment paper. Spread the rolled oats evenly on a baking sheet and bake for 15 to 20 minutes, until they are lightly colored and fragrant. Remove from the oven, transfer to a plate, and let cool to room temperature.

While the oats are cooling, coat a nonstick sauté pan with cooking spray. Heat the pan over medium-high heat, add the chopped apples, and cook for 3 minutes, or until they are tender. Scrape the apples into a large bowl and set aside for about 10 minutes to cool. Add the mashed bananas and apple juice to the cooked apples and stir with a wooden spoon to incorporate. In a separate bowl, combine the toasted oats, walnuts, dried apples, raisins, oat flour, ginger, cinnamon, cloves, mace, nutmeg, baking powder, and salt. Pour the wet ingredients into the dry ingredients and, using your hands or a large spoon, mix the dough together. Cover the bowl with plastic wrap and let the dough rest at room temperature for 10 minutes.

Using a ¾-ounce ice cream scoop, portion 12 scoops of cookie dough onto the silicone mat. Cover the scooped portions of dough with plastic wrap and, using the flat bottom of a glass, press down on the scoops until they are ½ inch thick. Place the cookies in the oven and bake for 12 to 15 minutes, until golden brown. Remove the baking sheet from the oven and set on a cooling rack to cool completely. The cookies will keep, stored in a plastic container or plastic bag, for up to 1 week.

MAKES 30 COOKIES

3 SMARTPOINTS PER COOKIE | 85 CALORIES

OMELETTE

Extra virgin olive oil cooking spray

¼ medium red bell pepper, cored, seeded, and finely diced

½ small scallion, thinly sliced

1 cup fresh spinach leaves, chopped

Sabatino truffle salt

Freshly ground black pepper

1 large egg

4 large egg whites

Sabatino Truffle Zest

1 slice reduced-fat pepper Jack cheese

1 tablespoon grated (on a Microplane) Parmesan cheese

Preheat the oven to 425°F.

Lightly coat a medium nonstick sauté pan with cooking spray and heat it over medium heat. Add the bell pepper and scallion and sauté until softened, about 5 minutes. Add the spinach and stir until wilted, about 1 minute. Season with truffle salt and pepper. Scrape the mixture onto a double layer of paper towels to absorb excess moisture.

In a small bowl, whisk together the egg and egg whites. Coat a medium nonstick ovenproof sauté pan with cooking spray and heat over medium-high heat. Pour the eggs into the pan and, using a silicone spatula, quickly stir the eggs around as if you were making scrambled eggs. As the eggs begin to come together, remove the pan from the heat and use your spatula to smooth the egg out to make an even layer. Season what will be the inside of the omelette with truffle salt, pepper, and Truffle Zest and place the Jack cheese on top. Press any excess moisture out of the vegetable mixture, then add it to the omelette in an even layer.

Place the open-face omelette in the oven and leave it just long enough for the cheese to melt and the eggs to set, 2 to 3 minutes. Remove the omelette from the oven and fold it: Hold the pan with the handle facing you and the opposite side tilting toward your plate. Using the spatula, lift the omelette and fold it onto itself, starting with the edge closest to the handle and continuing as the omelette makes its way onto the plate in a thin football shape. Sprinkle with the Parmesan and serve.

SERVES 1 | 6 SMARTPOINTS PER SERVING

258 CALORIES

ASPARAGUS AND GOAT CHEESE FRITTATA WITH SMOKED SALMON

Salt

1 bunch asparagus, woody ends snapped off and discarded

8 large eggs

½ cup whole milk

1 teaspoon Sabatino Truffle Zest

1 teaspoon Sabatino truffle salt

4 ounces soft goat cheese, at room temperature

2 teaspoons extra virgin olive oil

1 shallot, minced

½ teaspoon sea salt

¼ teaspoon freshly ground black pepper

2 tablespoons chopped fresh tarragon

¼ cup 2% plain Greek yogurt

2 teaspoons Sabatino white truffle oil

Zest of 1 lemon

8 ounces thinly sliced smoked salmon

¼ cup thinly sliced fresh chives

Preheat the oven to 350°F. Fill a large bowl with ice and water to make an ice-water bath. Fill a large saucepan with water and bring to a boil over high heat. Salt the water, then add the asparagus and boil until al dente, about 3 minutes, a little more or less depending on its thickness. Drain, then immediately transfer to the ice-water bath to stop the cooking. Leave for about a minute, until completely cooled, then drain again and pat dry with paper towels.

In a large bowl, whisk the eggs, then whisk in the milk, Truffle Zest, and ¾ teaspoon of the truffle salt until the Truffle Zest is dissolved. Crumble in the goat cheese and whisk or stir until the goat cheese is fully mixed into the eggs with small crumbles showing.

In a 10-inch cast-iron or ovenproof nonstick skillet, heat the olive oil over medium-high heat. Add the shallot and cook for about 2 minutes, until softened but not browned. Add the asparagus, sea salt, ¼ teaspoon black pepper, and the tarragon. Lower the heat to medium, pour the egg mixture into the pan, and cook without stirring until the edges begin to set, 5 to 7 minutes. Transfer the pan to the oven and bake until the egg is set and the frittata is puffy and golden on top, 12 to 15 minutes.

Meanwhile, in a small bowl, whisk together the yogurt, truffle oil, lemon zest, and the remaining ¼ teaspoon truffle salt.

Remove the skillet from the oven and let rest for 5 minutes. Spread the yogurt mixture all over the frittata. Slice into wedges, arrange the smoked salmon on top, and sprinkle the wedges with chives.

SERVES 8 | 5 SMARTPOINTS PER SERVING

180 CALORIES

7 $\frac{1}{2}$ MINUTE EGG

1 large egg
Sabatino truffle salt

Pour 1 quart water into a medium saucepan. Place over high heat and bring to a full rolling boil. Place the egg on a spoon or in a ladle and carefully submerge it into the pot. Reduce the heat to low, set a timer for 7 $\frac{1}{2}$ minutes, and cover the pot with the lid. Remove the pot from the heat, pour off the water, and run cold water over the egg while peeling it. Pat the egg dry with a paper towel and serve warm with truffle salt sprinkled on top

SERVES 1 | 2 SMARTPOINTS PER SERVING | 72 CALORIES

It's the salsa that makes it so sexy. Hot hot!

SEXY BREAKFAST

Breakfast Salsa

2 serrano chiles, stemmed

2 jalapeño chiles, stemmed

4 cloves garlic, peeled

¼ small white onion, peeled

2 medium Roma tomatoes

1 small tomato on the vine or cluster tomato

Salt

Scramble

1 large egg yolk

3 large egg whites

1 teaspoon water

Salt and freshly ground black pepper

Extra virgin olive oil cooking spray

1 large scallion, white and light green parts, finely chopped

To make the salsa: Preheat the broiler. Lay the chiles, garlic, onion, and tomatoes out on a broiler pan or baking sheet. Set the pan 4 inches from the heat source and broil for 5 to 6 minutes, until darkened in color and blackened in spots.

In a food processor, combine the chiles, garlic, onion, and a pinch of salt and pulse to a medium-fine chop. Add the tomatoes (you can add them whole, as they will be very soft) and process until all the ingredients are broken down and well combined. Season with salt and spoon into a bowl.

To make the scramble: In a medium bowl, whisk the egg yolk, egg whites, water, and a pinch of salt and pepper. Coat a medium nonstick skillet with cooking spray and heat over medium-high heat. Add the scallion and sauté for about 30 seconds, until softened, then add the eggs and, using a heatproof spatula, slowly mix until soft curds start to form. Continue to stir until the eggs are cooked through, about 1 ½ minutes total.

To serve: Spoon the eggs onto a plate and serve smothered in ¼ cup of salsa. Any leftover salsa will keep refrigerated for up to a week. Serve with sliced avocado and a slice of healthy toasted bread if you like.

SERVES 1 | 3 SMARTPOINTS PER SERVING
130 CALORIES

THE USUAL

Flesh of ¼ avocado
1 teaspoon fresh lemon juice, or to taste
Salt and freshly ground black pepper
1 slice whole-grain bread, toasted
2 slices tomato
2 ounces smoked turkey
2 fresh basil leaves
1 egg, cooked over medium

Place the avocado in a small bowl and
mash it with a fork. Add the lemon
juice and season with salt and pepper.
Spread the avocado over the bread.
Add the tomato slices, turkey, and
basil and top with the egg. Sprinkle on
a little salt and pepper and serve.

SERVES 1
7 SMARTPOINTS PER SERVING
281 CALORIES

Sunshine + fresh air + people you care about = happiness. Enjoying an outdoor meal with Thando, one of my South African "daughters."

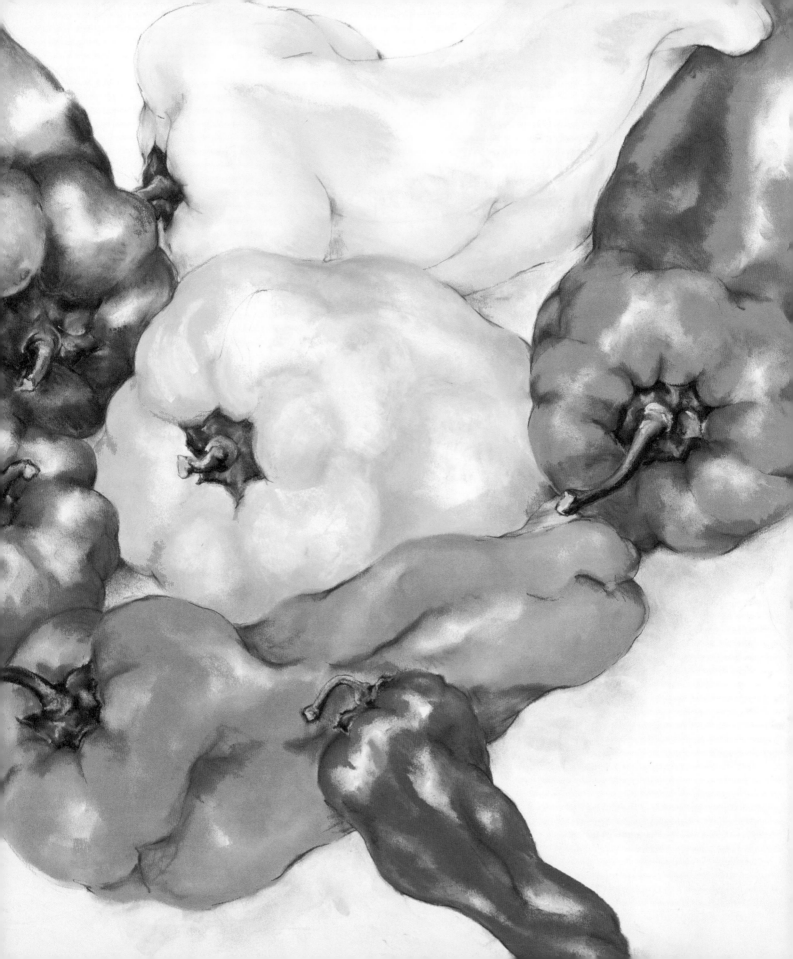

A WORLD OF POSSIBILITY

I'D NEVER BEEN TO INDIA. I WASN'T WELL-VERSED IN ITS CUSTOMS, ITS CULTURE, ITS GEOGRAPHY, ITS FLORA, ITS FAUNA— OR ITS FOOD.

So in 2012 I grabbed my *Next Chapter* team, my camera crew, my goddaughter, Kirby, and off we went to explore the world. I saw paradise and I saw poverty during my trip. In Jaipur, I was treated to the kind of luxury generally reserved for fairy tales, complete with painted elephants and bejeweled camels in the courtyard of a 300-room palace where I'd been invited to dine with royalty. The women wore jewel-toned silk saris and the men were every bit as elegant. The music was cinematic, the art and textiles were museum quality, and the night was beyond opulent. Everything was exquisite.

The Taj Mahal, described by Nobel
laureate Rabindranath Tagore as "the teardrop on the
cheek of time," is awesome and intimate and a very
long way from Koscinsko, Mississippi.
It's one of the most spectacular places I've ever been.
No wonder it's one of the seven wonders!

In the crowded slums of Mumbai, home to 10 million people, I met five who made a deep and lasting impression on me. Rajesh Hegde-Ray and his wife, Parvati, ate, slept, prayed, and raised their three daughters—six-year-old twins and their 12-year-old big sister—in a single concrete-walled room that measured no more than 10 feet by 10 feet. What can I say about this family? They had only themselves to give, and they gave with open hearts. They shared their time, they shared their goodness, and they shared one more unforgettable gift: masala chai.

As we sat together on the floor, Parvati reached behind the scrap of cloth that curtained off most of her family's possessions, pulled out a simple tea set, and watched as Rajesh proceeded to brew the most transporting cup of tea I'd ever tasted. Was it the pungent mix of spices or the Hegde-Rays' kind welcome that made it so distinctive? We sipped, we talked, and eventually we hugged our goodbyes. As I write this now, it occurs to me that just as I'd left Jaipur feeling honored to experience a night of opulence and pageantry, it was also an honor to witness a family of five laughing together, supporting each other, and functioning in harmony under circumstances most Americans would find hard to comprehend. Equally an honor, and equally delightful.

When I look back on that trip, I think of the soft pink light, the lyrical voices, the chaotic traffic, the people who seemed to wish everyone well, and the food. The first time I tasted Indian food was...in India! It was a revelation, starting with—you guessed it—the bread. Naan is a traditional flatbread, an unpretentious, warm, pillowy, puffy, chewy, heavenly flatbread, sort of like if pizza dough and a buttermilk biscuit got together and did their thing. The waiter brought us garlic naan and it was love at first bite. All I could do was keep asking for more, and

Sharing chai with the Hegde-Ray family in 2012. Their home is small on space but large on love.

more, until another waiter, equal parts alarmed and concerned, approached the table to ask, "Madam, should we cancel your meal?"

I came back from that trip wanting to bring naan and tea into my life at home—plus so many other spectacular dishes from around the globe. I now own a tandoor oven for baking naan, and I'm delighted to say I've mastered the art of chai.

I've come to understand that there's a beauty, a sense of order, in the tea-making process. I wake up every day, I meditate, I take in the silence, and then I start the chai. As it steeps, my head clears; as the flavors develop, my thoughts come into focus. I get centered, I get calm. I get prepared for whatever the day is going to bring. I become aware of how the steam swirls and disappears; the woodsy, citrusy, spicy, floral fragrance; the way the translucent amber color slowly turns creamy beige with the almond milk. I spoon a stiff dollop of foam on top, and feel the warmth of the mug in my hands.

Next comes a cup for Stedman—I've got him hooked, too. As the morning unfolds, I'm often making chai for the folks who work with me, and anyone who happens by the front gate—"Hey repairman, UPS guy, want a cuppa chai?" I'm trying to carry on the spirit of hospitality, humility, and generosity that the Hegde-Rays greeted me with in their love-filled home. It feels like an act of grace to share a cup of tea with people, whatever language they speak, however they make their way in the world. If India taught me anything, it's that we all want the same things: health, happiness, and a solid connection to our own humanity.

The recipes in this chapter celebrate the rich history and culture, the colors and flavors, and above all, the people of India, Vietnam, Thailand, and Japan. I hope when you start to cook, you'll pause to do what I always do now: think for a moment of the beauty of the rituals in your life, and make room for one more person at your table. *Namaste.*

Meditation refreshes my mind, realigns my spirit, and returns me to myself again! It's the key to clarity!

I love tea so much I came back and now make my own chai. Tea is one beverage you can drink all day, and it won't cost you a point.

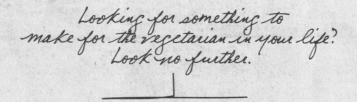

Looking for something to make for the vegetarian in your life? Look no further.

INDIAN PUMPKIN CURRY

This recipe is so nourishing that I keep thinking it must be what Indian grandmothers make when somebody has a cold! Pumpkins, they aren't just about pie and jack-o'-lanterns anymore!

INGREDIENTS:

1 tablespoon coconut oil

1 large onion, finely chopped

3 garlic cloves, grated on a Microplane

2 tablespoons minced ginger

Seeds of 3 cardamom pods

½ teaspoon black mustard seeds

1 teaspoon ground cumin

1 tablespoon ground coriander

1 teaspoon ground turmeric

2 teaspoons garam masala

2 Kashmiri chiles or arbol chiles

1 (2-pound) pumpkin or winter squash, peeled, seeds removed, and cut into ¾-inch cubes

2 teaspoons salt

1 cup Vegetable Stock (page 42), plus more if needed

1 (14-ounce) can light coconut milk

1 (15-ounce) can chickpeas, drained and rinsed

Freshly ground black pepper

Large handful fresh mint leaves, chopped

Large handful fresh cilantro leaves, chopped

Lime wedges

Naan (page 122)

DIRECTIONS:

Heat the oil in a large, heavy-bottom pot over medium-high heat. Add the onions and cook for about 5 minutes, until softened. Add the garlic and ginger and cook for about 1 minute, until fragrant. Add the cardamom seeds, mustard seeds, cumin, coriander, turmeric, garam masala, and chiles and cook, stirring, until aromatic, about 1 minute, adding a tiny bit of water if the mixture starts to stick to the bottom of the pan. Add the pumpkin or squash, salt, vegetable stock, and coconut milk, bring to a simmer, then reduce the heat to medium-low and simmer until the pumpkin is starting to soften, about 20 minutes.

Add the chickpeas and simmer for an additional 10 minutes, or until the pumpkin is fully softened. Season with pepper, spoon into bowls, and serve topped with the mint and cilantro and with lime wedges and naan alongside.

PREP TIME	COOK TIME	SERVES	SmartPoints	CALORIES
15 MINUTES	**1** HOUR	**6**	**6** PER SERVING	**216** PER SERVING

MOREL PILAU

RECIPE INSPIRED BY RICK STEIN

I first tried this rice pilaf dish in the Kashmiri region of India. The exotic spices—garam masala, ginger, cardamom, cumin, to name just a few—always remind me that there are a whole lot of extraordinary dishes in the world and that, really, nothing connects us quite like sharing food.

You could also use brown rice.

INGREDIENTS:

½ ounce dried morel mushrooms

1 ¾ cups hot water

1 cup white basmati rice

1 tablespoon vegetable oil

½ teaspoon garam masala

1 medium yellow onion, finely chopped

1-inch piece ginger, grated on a Microplane

3 cloves garlic, grated on a Microplane

¾ teaspoon salt

Handful of fresh cilantro leaves, chopped

1 to 3 small green chiles, chopped

DIRECTIONS:

Put the morels in a medium bowl and cover with the hot water. Place a small plate or bowl on top of the morels to keep them submerged in the water and let them sit for 30 minutes to reconstitute. Fish the morels out of the water and place them in a separate bowl. Strain the soaking liquid through a fine-mesh strainer into a separate bowl.

Meanwhile, place the rice in a medium bowl, add cold water to cover by about an inch, and leave to soak for 30 minutes, then drain and rinse.

Heat the oil in a heavy-bottom saucepan over medium heat. Add the garam masala and cook, swirling it around in the oil for about 30 seconds, until aromatic. Add the onion and cook until softened and starting to brown, about 7 minutes. Add the ginger and garlic and cook, stirring, for about 2 minutes, until aromatic. Add the drained rice, increase the heat to high, and cook, stirring, for 1 minute to coat the rice in the oil. Add the rehydrated morels, the reserved morel soaking water, and the salt, and bring to a boil. Reduce the heat to medium-low, cover, and cook for 15 minutes. Turn off the heat and leave for 10 minutes, then fluff with a fork. Transfer to a serving bowl, sprinkle with the cilantro and green chiles, and serve.

In India, the morels are called Suchi.

PREP TIME	COOK TIME	SERVES	SMARTPOINTS	CALORIES
15 MINUTES	30 MINUTES	4	6 PER SERVING	220 PER SERVING

NAAN

There's something very moving, even romantic, about tasting a dish knowing that people have been eating that same dish for centuries. No matter where you're from, bread is the thing that connects us all. If anything's going to make you fall truly, madly, deeply, head over heels in love with Indian food, this is it!

INGREDIENTS:

2 cups all-purpose flour, plus more as needed

1½ tablespoons ground caraway

1 teaspoon salt

¾ cup milk

1½ teaspoons honey

¼ ounce (½ packet) active dry yeast

1½ tablespoons liquid coconut oil, plus more for the bowl

½ cup nonfat Greek yogurt

DIRECTIONS:

In a large bowl, whisk together the flour, caraway, and salt. In a small saucepan, heat the milk over medium heat until it reaches 90°F. Stir in the honey to dissolve it, then add the yeast and leave for about 5 minutes, until it is frothy. Add the oil and yogurt to the flour, followed by the warm milk mixture, and gradually mix everything together to make a soft dough, adding a little warm water if the dough is looking dry or a little more flour if it's looking wet.

Lightly flour a work surface, turn the dough out onto it, and knead for about 5 minutes, until smooth and only slightly sticky, adding more flour if the dough starts to stick. Return the dough to a clean, lightly oiled bowl, turning to coat all sides. Cover with a clean kitchen towel and leave in a warm spot for about 1 hour, until doubled in size.

Heat a large cast-iron skillet over medium-high heat.

Punch down the dough, cut it into 1-ounce pieces, and roll the pieces into balls. On a lightly floured work surface and using a lightly floured rolling pin, roll the balls into 7-inch-long, ⅛-inch-thick rounds, adding more flour while rolling if necessary, then stretch one end to make a rough teardrop shape. Working with one piece at a time, add the naan to the pan and sear until it starts to puff up and char on the bottom, 1 to 2 minutes. Flip the naan and cook for another 1 to 2 minutes, until charred on the second side. Continue rolling out dough and cooking naan, wrapping the finished naan in a kitchen towel–lined basket as each is done to keep it warm.

PREP TIME	COOK TIME	SERVES	SMARTPOINTS	CALORIES
30 MINUTES (PLUS 1-2 HOURS FOR DOUGH TO REST)	4 MINUTES EACH	20	2 PER SERVING	68 PER SERVING

DRY PRAWN CURRY

Don't you love a one-dish wonder? This recipe is fast and easy and requires hardly any cleanup. It also contains coconut oil, ginger, and turmeric—not only exotic but also terrifically good for body and soul.

INGREDIENTS:

2 tablespoons coconut oil

1 pound large shrimp, peeled and deveined

Salt

1 tablespoon finely chopped ginger

4 fresh green chiles, with seeds, cut in half lengthwise, each half cut into thirds

4 shallots, thinly sliced

2 dried Kashmiri chiles, torn into pieces

6 curry leaves

1 cup fresh or thawed frozen grated coconut

¼ teaspoon ground turmeric

2 teaspoons tamarind concentrate dissolved in ¼ cup water

Be careful when cooking the shrimp. Cook an extra minute or two and they'll turn to rubber!

DIRECTIONS:

In a large skillet, heat 1 tablespoon of the oil over medium-high heat. Season the shrimp with salt and add them to the pan in a single layer. Cook for about 2 minutes, until they start to turn pink on the underside, then use tongs to flip them and cook for another 2 minutes, or until they start to turn pink on the second side. Remove the shrimp to a plate.

Add the remaining 1 tablespoon oil to the skillet, then add the ginger, green chiles, and shallots and cook, stirring constantly, until they start to soften and brown, about 3 minutes. Add the Kashmiri chiles and curry leaves and cook, stirring constantly, for 1 minute, or until the shallots and ginger are well browned. Add the coconut and turmeric and cook, stirring constantly, for about 3 minutes, until the coconut is well browned. Add the tamarind, season with salt, and cook, stirring constantly, for about 3 minutes, until the liquid is absorbed and the coconut goes from soft to crisp. Return the shrimp to the pan and cook, stirring constantly, for about 2 minutes, until it is fully pink and cooked through and well coated in the coconut. Taste and add more salt if needed. Spoon into bowls and serve.

PREP TIME	COOK TIME	SERVES	SmartPoints	CALORIES
15 MINUTES	10–15 MINUTES	6	5 PER SERVING	157 PER SERVING

GRILLED SHRIMP LETTUCE WRAPS WITH SWEET CHILI SAUCE, MANGO, AND TOASTED COCONUT

Here is the perfect summer recipe. I like to assemble it right before it's time to serve. Just place the shrimp on a large platter with the lettuce leaves, a bowl of mango, and a side of toasted coconut. Let your guests make their own lettuce wraps and enjoy!

INGREDIENTS:

1 pound large shrimp, peeled and deveined

1 tablespoon liquid coconut oil

1 teaspoon sea salt

½ cup Thai sweet chili sauce, plus more for serving

Zest and juice of 2 limes

1 cup unsweetened flaked coconut

2 mangoes, peeled, pitted, and cut into small dice

¼ cup chopped fresh chives

½ cup chopped fresh cilantro leaves

1 head butter lettuce, leaves separated

DIRECTIONS:

Preheat the oven to 350°F. Place the shrimp in a large bowl and toss with the oil and salt. Add the sweet chili sauce and half of the lime zest and set aside to marinate at room temperature for 10 minutes.

Place the coconut on a baking sheet and toast for 8 to 10 minutes, until lightly colored, keeping a close watch on it, as it can burn quickly. Remove from the oven and transfer to a plate to cool.

Heat a grill or grill pan to medium-high. Add the shrimp in one layer and cook until nicely browned on the bottom, about 3 minutes. Using tongs, flip the shrimp and cook until browned all over and cooked through, about another 3 minutes. Transfer the shrimp to a serving bowl.

Place the mango in a small bowl and add the remaining lime zest, the lime juice, chives, and cilantro.

Put the lettuce leaves onto a platter. Pour some sweet chili sauce into a small dipping bowl. Set out bowls with the mango and the toasted coconut, and invite your guests to assemble their wraps self-serve-style.

PREP TIME	COOK TIME	SERVES	SmartPoints	CALORIES
15 MINUTES	10 MINUTES	8	6 PER SERVING	201 PER SERVING

CHICKEN TIKKA MASALA
WITH BROWN BASMATI RICE

If there's one dish guaranteed to show up at every Indian restaurant, this is it.
Sometimes when I have it with naan bread, it's kind of like having Indian pizza!

INGREDIENTS:

Chicken marinade

3 cloves garlic, minced

1-inch piece ginger, minced

¼ medium yellow onion, minced

Juice of 1 lime

1 teaspoon ground cumin

1 teaspoon ground coriander

¼ teaspoon ground cayenne

2 teaspoons paprika

3 tablespoons nonfat Greek yogurt

1 teaspoon kosher salt

2 pounds boneless, skinless chicken thighs, cut into 1 ½-inch cubes

Sauce

1 teaspoon ghee or canola oil

¼ medium red onion, sliced

½-inch piece ginger, minced

4 cloves garlic, minced

1 teaspoon ground coriander

1 teaspoon ground cumin

1 teaspoon crushed red pepper flakes

1 bay leaf

2 cups Pomi strained tomatoes

¼ cup heavy cream

Salt

2 teaspoons fresh lime juice, or to taste

Brown Basmati Rice

1 cup brown basmati rice

½ teaspoon ghee or canola oil

4 whole cloves

1 cup water or Great Chicken Stock (page 42)

½ teaspoon fine sea salt

DIRECTIONS:

To marinate the chicken: Combine all the marinade ingredients in a large bowl, add the chicken, and stir to fully coat. Place in the refrigerator and marinate for 2 hours, stirring a couple of times.

To roast the chicken: Preheat the broiler. Place the chicken on a roasting pan, removing most of the marinade, and broil until it starts to blacken in spots, about 10 minutes (it's OK if the chicken is not cooked through; it will finish cooking in the sauce).

To make the sauce and finish the chicken: Heat the ghee in a large saucepan over medium-high heat. Add the onion and cook, stirring often, until well browned, about 5 minutes. Add the ginger, garlic, coriander, cumin, red pepper flakes, and bay leaf and cook, stirring, for about 1 minute, until aromatic, adding a tiny bit of water if the mixture starts to stick to the pan. Add the tomatoes, bring to a simmer, then reduce the heat and cook for 15 minutes. Add the chicken and cream, return to a simmer, and cook for 15 minutes. Remove the bay leaf, season with salt, stir in the lime juice, and serve over rice.

To make the rice: Preheat the oven to 350°F. Place the rice in a strainer and rinse it under cold running water. Shake to drain it well. Heat the ghee in a medium ovenproof saucepan over medium heat. Add the cloves and toast for about 1 minute, until aromatic. Add the rice and toast, stirring often, for 1 to 2 minutes, until lightly colored and aromatic. Add the water and salt and bring to a simmer. Cover, place in the oven, and cook for 40 minutes, or until all the water is absorbed. Remove the pan from the oven, let rest with the cover on for 10 minutes, then fluff the rice and serve.

PREP TIME	COOK TIME	SERVES	SmartPoints	CALORIES
30 MINUTES (PLUS 2 HRS FOR MARINATE)	**40** MINUTES	**6**	**10** PER SERVING	**425** PER SERVING

VIETNAMESE CHICKEN SALAD

This is the perfect blend of color and texture, lightness and substance. And it's really pretty
on the plate, so if what they say about the first taste being with the eyes is true,
you're going to love this even before taking a bite.

INGREDIENTS:

Salad

4 boneless, skinless chicken breasts

1 teaspoon salt, or to taste

4 cups shredded Napa cabbage

4 scallions, thinly sliced diagonally

2 cups thinly sliced sugar snap peas

3 medium carrots, thinly sliced diagonally
and cut into matchsticks

1 red bell pepper, cored, seeded,
and thinly sliced

1/2 cup fresh mint leaves, torn into pieces

1/2 cup fresh cilantro leaves, torn into pieces

1/2 cup roasted cashews, roughly chopped

1 tablespoon black sesame seeds

Dressing

1/3 cup fresh lime juice, or to taste

1 serrano chile, seeded and minced

3 cloves garlic, grated on a Microplane

1-inch piece ginger, grated on a Microplane

1 tablespoon agave nectar

3 tablespoons fish sauce

1 tablespoon toasted sesame oil

DIRECTIONS:

To poach the chicken, place the breasts in a
medium saucepan, add water to cover by 2 inches,
then add 1/2 teaspoon salt. Place over medium-high
heat and bring just to a simmer, then reduce the
heat and cook at a very low simmer for about 15
minutes, until the breasts are cooked through and
they reach a temperature of 160°F as measured on
an instant-read thermometer. Remove the chicken
from the poaching liquid to a cutting board, cool
completely, then shred the chicken using your
fingers or two forks.

To compose the salad, in a large salad bowl, toss
the cabbage, scallions, sugar snap peas, carrots, and
bell pepper with remaining salt. In a separate bowl,
whisk together all the dressing ingredients, then
toss well with the vegetables. Let sit for 10 minutes,
then add the shredded chicken and toss to coat.
Taste and add more salt or lime juice if needed. Mix
in the mint and cilantro, top with the cashews and
sesame seeds, and serve.

PREP TIME	COOK TIME	SERVES	SmartPoints	CALORIES
25 MINUTES	15 MINUTES	6 MAKES ABOUT 12 CUPS	6 PER SERVING	251 PER SERVING

Fresh mint makes everything better!

There's something very festive about this dish—
it tastes like a holiday just waiting to be celebrated.

INDIAN-SPICED APRICOT CHICKEN

RECIPE INSPIRED BY RICK STEIN

If you or your guests haven't experienced much Indian food, this is a perfect introduction to the cuisine. People won't necessarily be able to identify all the different spices— they'll only know they want more than one helping!

INGREDIENTS:

1½ teaspoons ground Kashmiri chile

1 teaspoon ground cumin

1 teaspoon ground coriander

1 teaspoon garam masala

½ teaspoon ground turmeric

½ teaspoon ground cinnamon

½ teaspoon ground cayenne

¼ teaspoon ground cardamom

¼ teaspoon ground cloves

¼ teaspoon cracked black pepper

1 teaspoon salt, plus more if needed

1 (3½-pound) chicken, cut into 8 pieces, skin removed

2 tablespoons extra virgin olive oil

1 medium onion, finely chopped

1-inch piece ginger, peeled and grated

3 cloves garlic, peeled and chopped

4 medium plum tomatoes, seeds removed, finely chopped

2 tablespoons white wine vinegar

1 teaspoon brown sugar

¾ cup dried apricots, quartered

Leaves and tender stems of ½ bunch cilantro

DIRECTIONS:

Preheat the oven to 375°F. In a small bowl, combine the ground Kashmiri chile, cumin, coriander, garam masala, turmeric, cinnamon, cayenne, cardamom, cloves, and black pepper. Season the chicken all over with half of the spice mixture and ½ teaspoon of the salt.

In a large ovenproof sauté pan, heat the oil over medium-high heat. Add the onion and cook, stirring often, until lightly browned, about 5 minutes. Add the ginger and garlic and cook until fragrant, about 2 minutes. Add the chicken to the pan and cook for 3 to 4 minutes on each side, until lightly browned all over. Add the remaining half of the spice mixture, the tomatoes, vinegar, brown sugar, apricots, and the remaining ½ teaspoon salt. Add water to cover the chicken three-quarters of the way. Bring the mixture to a boil, cover, and turn off the heat. Place the pan in the oven and bake for 30 to 40 minutes, until an instant-read thermometer inserted into a breast reads 165°F.

Remove the pan from the oven. Using tongs, remove the chicken pieces from the pan to a serving bowl. Return the pan to the stovetop, place over high heat, and cook uncovered until the sauce is thickened, about 10 minutes. Stir in the cilantro and serve.

PREP TIME	COOK TIME	SERVES	SMARTPOINTS	CALORIES
20 MINUTES	30-40 MINUTES	4	9 PER SERVING	373 PER SERVING

The dressing also tastes delicious over drained canned albacore tuna if fresh fish is unavailable.

PEPPERED TUNA

The low-fat salad dressing in this dish is so good drizzled over everything from noodles
to chicken to green beans that I sometimes take it with me when I go out to eat.
I also like keeping a supply in the fridge.

Mirin is cooking wine; look for it in the Asian section of your supermarket.

INGREDIENTS:

Spicy Sesame Ginger Dressing

1 tablespoon toasted sesame oil

3 tablespoons soy sauce or tamari

1 ½ tablespoons grated (on a Microplane) fresh ginger

3 tablespoons rice vinegar

1 tablespoon mirin

1 tablespoon chopped shallot

1 tablespoon chopped seeded jalapeño chile

1 tablespoon honey

Fish

12 ounces fresh, sashimi-grade albacore or ahi tuna (see Note), in a single rectangular piece

½ teaspoon salt

1 tablespoon coarsely ground black pepper

1 ½ tablespoons tan or black sesame seeds

1 tablespoon toasted sesame oil

3 small cucumbers, sliced

4 radishes, sliced

1 cup microgreens or sunflower sprouts

¼ cup chopped scallions

DIRECTIONS:

To make the dressing: Combine the toasted sesame oil, soy sauce or tamari, ginger, vinegar, mirin, shallot, jalapeño, and honey in a blender and blend until smooth.

To cook the fish: Sprinkle the tuna on both sides with the salt. On a large flat plate, combine the black pepper and sesame seeds and gently press the fish into the mixture.

Heat the toasted sesame oil in a large skillet over medium-high heat. Add the fish and sear both sides, about 1 minute per side for rare, or to desired doneness. Remove to a cutting board and thinly slice the fish against the grain.

Arrange the cucumber slices, radish slices, and microgreens on a serving plate to make a bed for the fish. Add the fish and garnish with the scallions. Drizzle ¼ cup of the dressing on top, reserving the rest for another recipe. Serve immediately.

Note: Drained canned albacore tuna packed in water can be used as a substitute for the fresh fish.

PREP TIME	COOK TIME	SERVES	SmartPoints	CALORIES
20 MINUTES	7 MINUTES	4	4 PER SERVING	186 PER SERVING

THAI RED CURRY WITH SHRIMP
AND PINEAPPLE

I love the incredible layers of flavor in this recipe. It's bright, spicy, slightly sweet, and full of freshness.

INGREDIENTS:

1 tablespoon coconut oil

1-inch piece ginger, grated on a Microplane

2 shallots, minced

3 scallions, white parts only, chopped

2 cloves garlic, minced

1 serrano chile, seeds removed and thinly sliced

3 tablespoons prepared red curry paste, such as Thai Kitchen brand

1 (14-ounce) can unsweetened light coconut milk

2 teaspoons Thai fish sauce

2 teaspoons agave nectar

1½ pounds large shrimp, peeled and deveined

1 cup thinly sliced (on the diagonal) sugar snap peas

1 red bell pepper, cored, seeded, and julienned

1 yellow bell pepper, cored, seeded, and julienned

1 medium zucchini, cut into ¼-inch cubes

Up to ½ cup Vegetable Stock (page 42)

1 cup fresh or thawed frozen peas

1 cup cubed (½-inch cubes) fresh pineapple

Zest and juice of 1 lime, or to taste

Sea salt

Garnishes

Finely chopped fresh chives

Finely chopped fresh Thai basil

Whole fresh cilantro leaves

Steamed rice for serving (optional)

DIRECTIONS:

In a large sauté pan, heat the oil over medium heat. Add the ginger, shallots, scallions, garlic, and chile and cook for about 5 minutes, stirring often, until the shallots are softened. Add the red curry paste and cook, stirring often, for an additional 4 minutes, adding a tiny bit of water if the paste starts to stick to the bottom of the pan.

Pour in the coconut milk, fish sauce, and agave and bring to a simmer. Add the shrimp, sugar snap peas, bell pepper, and zucchini, and return to a simmer. Reduce the heat to medium-low and cook for 8 minutes, or until the shrimp is cooked through and the vegetables are crisp-tender, adding some vegetable stock if needed to keep all the ingredients moist. Add the peas, pineapple, and lime zest and juice and season with salt. Remove from heat and stir in the herb garnishes. Serve over rice if you like.

PREP TIME	COOK TIME	SERVES	SMARTPOINTS	CALORIES
30 MINUTES	30 MINUTES	6	6 PER SERVING	253 PER SERVING

PINEAPPLE FRIED RICE

Colorful, tangy, and easy to throw together, this dish has a slightly tropical taste
thanks to the pineapple, and that little hit of lime adds a nice bright flavor.

INGREDIENTS:

1 tablespoon toasted sesame oil

¼ cup chopped yellow onion

2 cloves garlic, minced

2 tablespoons diced carrot

½ cup diced fresh pineapple

3 cups cooked and cooled white rice
(day-old is fine)

1 ½ tablespoons fish sauce

1 ½ tablespoons soy sauce

1 teaspoon freshly ground white pepper

2 large eggs, beaten

2 tablespoons fresh or thawed frozen peas

Salt

2 tablespoons thinly sliced scallions

1 tablespoon chopped fresh cilantro

Juice of 1 lime

DIRECTIONS:

Heat the oil in a large nonstick skillet over medium heat. Add the onion and cook for about 5 minutes, until starting to soften, then add the garlic and cook for another minute, or until aromatic. Stir in the carrot and pineapple, then add the rice and stir well. Stir in the fish sauce, soy sauce, and white pepper, increase the heat to medium-high, and continue to cook, stirring, for 2 minutes.

Using a spatula, push the rice to the sides of the pan to make a large "well" in the middle of the fried rice. Pour the beaten eggs in the well, leave for about 30 seconds, then cover the eggs with the fried rice. Leave for 30 seconds to 1 minute, then continue to cook, stirring, until the egg is fully set and is incorporated into the fried rice, another minute or so. Add the peas, cook till warm throughout, season with salt if needed, then stir in the scallions, cilantro, and lime juice and serve.

PREP TIME	COOK TIME	SERVES	SmartPoints	CALORIES
20	15	6	4	163
MINUTES	MINUTES		PER SERVING	PER SERVING

Use the leftover pineapple to sweeten up plain yogurt.

I love this dish so much, I eat it as a complete meal.

JAPANESE BROWN RICE WITH KALE, AVOCADO, AND EDAMAME SALAD

RECIPE FROM PAULA NEL

I know this salad has more points than some of the others, but that's a small price to pay for all the nutrients you're getting. For example: One half cup of edamame (Japanese boiled or steamed soy beans) has 9 grams of protein and almost as much fiber as it does carbohydrates. It also contains around 10 percent of the daily value for vitamin A. And it's high in iron to boot— it contains about as much as a 4-ounce roasted chicken breast.

INGREDIENTS:

Dashi Stock

4 cups water

1 (4-inch) piece kombu seaweed

1 cup bonito flakes

Rice Salad

2 cups short-grain Japanese brown rice

Salt

3 cloves garlic, thinly sliced

3 tablespoons extra virgin olive oil

2 cups roughly chopped kale leaves

1 cup cooked edamame

¼ cup toasted pumpkin seeds

¼ cup toasted sunflower seeds

¼ cup toasted sesame seeds

2 tablespoons light soy sauce, or to taste

1 tablespoon yuzu juice or lemon juice, or to taste

2 scallions, white and light green parts, sliced

1 ripe avocado, cut in half, pit removed, and flesh sliced from the skin

DIRECTIONS:

To make the dashi stock: In a large saucepan, combine the water and kombu over medium-high heat and bring to a low simmer. Immediately reduce the heat to low and simmer for 10 minutes. Remove the pot from the heat and add the bonito flakes. Cover and set aside for 15 minutes to steep the bonito flakes. Strain the dashi through a fine-mesh strainer into a bowl and discard the kombu and bonito flakes.

To make the rice: Rinse out the pan you cooked the dashi stock in, return the stock to the pan, and bring to a boil over medium-high heat. Add the rice and 1 teaspoon salt, return to a simmer, then reduce the heat to low, cover, and cook until the water is absorbed and the rice is cooked through, about 45 minutes. Remove from the heat and leave the lid on for 10 minutes, then fluff with a fork, transfer to a serving bowl, and cool to room temperature.

While the rice is cooking, make the garlic oil: In a very small pot (a sturdy stainless steel measuring cup works well) or skillet, combine the garlic and oil. Place over low heat, bring to a low simmer, and cook for about 5 minutes, until it is lightly browned and fragrant.

To assemble the salad: Place the kale in a medium bowl, add a pinch of salt, and rub the kale between your fingers for a minute or two, until slightly wilted. Add the kale to the rice, then stir in the garlic and its oil, the edamame, most of the pumpkin seeds, sunflower seeds, and sesame seeds (reserving a little for garnish), the soy sauce, yuzu or lemon juice, and scallions. Season with salt and pepper and fold in the avocado just before serving. Spoon into bowls and serve with the reserved seeds sprinkled on top.

PREP TIME	COOK TIME	SERVES	SmartPoints	CALORIES
20 MINUTES	10 MINUTES	8	9 PER SERVING	332 PER SERVING

VELVET SHRIMP WITH CARROT GINGER PUREE AND TAMARIND ONION CARAMEL

What do Chinese restaurants know that a lot of home cooks do not? It's called velveting! This is a technique unique to Chinese cuisine that gives meat and seafood a juicy, delectable consistency.

INGREDIENTS:

Carrot Ginger Puree
1 pound carrots, thinly sliced
1 1/2 cups carrot juice
1 tablespoon grated (on a Microplane) ginger
1/2 teaspoon salt

Shrimp and marinade
1 pound medium shrimp, peeled and deveined
2 tablespoons cornstarch
1 teaspoon ground white pepper
1 teaspoon onion powder
1/2 teaspoon salt
1/4 cup Shaoxing wine or dry sherry
2 teaspoons grated (on a Microplane) ginger
2 teaspoons grated (on a Microplane) garlic

Tamarind Onion Caramel
1 tablespoon tamarind concentrate
1/2 medium yellow onion, chopped
1/4 cup fish sauce
1/4 cup carrot juice
2 cloves garlic, grated on a Microplane
1 1/2 cups sugar

Coating and frying the shrimp
2 large egg whites
1/2 teaspoon salt
2 tablespoons cornstarch
1/2 cup canola oil

Garnishes
Julienne slices of multicolored carrots
Thinly sliced scallion greens
Fresh cilantro leaves

DIRECTIONS:

To make the carrot ginger puree: Combine the carrots, carrot juice, ginger, and salt in a medium saucepan. Place over medium-high heat and bring to a boil. Reduce the heat to medium-low and simmer, stirring often, for 25 minutes, or until the carrots are very tender.

Strain the carrots and reserve the cooking liquid. Transfer the carrots to a blender and blend until smooth, stopping to scrape down the sides of the machine as needed and adding some of the reserved cooking liquid, 1 tablespoon at a time, to achieve a puree consistency.

While the carrots are cooking, marinate the shrimp: Rinse the shrimp under cold running water, drain, and blot dry with paper towels. In a medium bowl, whisk together the cornstarch, white pepper, onion powder, and salt. Whisk in the wine, then add the ginger and garlic. Add the shrimp and toss to coat in the marinade. Place in the refrigerator to marinate for up to 30 minutes.

While the shrimp is marinating, make the tamarind onion caramel: In a blender, combine the tamarind concentrate, onion, 1/4 cup water, the fish sauce, and carrot juice and blend until smooth. Add the garlic.

Combine the sugar with 1/4 cup water in a small, heavy saucepan such as an enameled cast-iron pan. Place over medium-low heat and leave undisturbed for about 3 minutes, until the sugar has dissolved, brushing off any sugar crystals that form on the sides with a wet pastry brush.

Continue to cook, occasionally swirling, not stirring, the pot to keep the mixture moving. The mixture will start to bubble and deepen in color. Once the caramel is a medium-dark

PREP TIME	COOK TIME	SERVES	SMARTPOINTS	CALORIES
30 MINUTES	1 HOUR	6	10 PER SERVING	324 PER SERVING

The caramel is spicy, savory, rich, and sweet. Feel free to make a batch to drizzle over chicken too!

amber color, 5 to 7 minutes, add the tamarind mixture and remove from the heat. It will bubble furiously. After the bubbling subsides, return the pan to medium-low heat and cook for 10 minutes, or until the caramel is the consistency of runny honey. If the caramel threatens to boil over, remove it from the heat for a few seconds until it goes back down. Note that the caramel will continue to thicken as it cools. Leftover caramel can be stored in the refrigerator, reheated to thin it, and used as a marinade for chicken or seafood.

To coat and fry the shrimp: Place the egg whites and salt in an electric mixer and mix on low speed until frothy. Add the cornstarch and continue to mix, slowly increasing the speed to medium, until the whites form soft to medium peaks. Drain the shrimp from the marinade, add the shrimp to the whites, and fold lightly to coat.

Set a wire rack atop a baking sheet. Heat the oil in a wok or large skillet over medium heat. Using tongs, add the shrimp, one at a time, being careful of spattering oil. Cook on each side for about 2 minutes, until browned and cooked through. As the shrimp are done, use tongs to place them on the wire rack. If the shrimp are finished before the other components are, keep them warm in a 200°F oven.

To serve: Arrange the shrimp on plates, add a scoop of the carrot ginger puree, drizzle with 1 to 1½ tablespoons caramel, and serve topped with the garnishes.

THAI GREEN CHICKEN CURRY

Toasting your spices to make the curry sauce may be an extra step, but it's a step well worth taking. It not only scents your kitchen, it really revs up all of the flavors.

INGREDIENTS:

Curry paste
MAKES ABOUT 1 CUP

1 tablespoon coriander seeds

1 ½ teaspoons cumin seeds

½ teaspoon white peppercorns

2 tablespoons thinly sliced fresh cilantro stems

1 ½ tablespoons chopped fresh galangal

1 ½ tablespoons chopped fresh ginger

¼ cup chopped garlic

1 kaffir lime leaf, torn into pieces

¼ cup sliced fresh lemongrass

1 tablespoon kosher salt

½ cup sliced shallots

1 teaspoon shrimp paste

4 green Thai bird chiles, stemmed and chopped

4 jalapeño chiles, stemmed and chopped

2 serrano chiles, stemmed and chopped

Curry

1 tablespoon coconut oil

1 red onion, chopped

2 tablespoons minced garlic

2 kaffir lime leaves

¼ cup green curry paste (see above)

1 pound boneless, skinless chicken breasts or thighs, cut into bite-size pieces

1 (14.5-ounce) can light coconut milk

1 red bell pepper, cored, seeded, and chopped

1 yellow bell pepper, cored, seeded, and chopped

½ cup chopped (1-inch pieces) asparagus

½ cup chopped (1-inch pieces) green beans

1 cup chopped bok choy

4 cups fresh spinach leaves

1 ½ tablespoons fish sauce, or to taste

1 tablespoon coconut sugar (optional)

DIRECTIONS:

To make the curry paste: Heat a small skillet over medium heat. Add the coriander seeds, cumin seeds, and peppercorns and toast, stirring often, until aromatic and the seeds turn a couple of shades darker. Remove from the skillet to a plate to cool briefly.

Combine all of the ingredients in a mini food processor and blitz to a paste. The paste will keep in a lidded container in the refrigerator for up to 3 weeks or in the freezer for up to 2 months.

To make the curry: Heat the oil in a large saucepan over medium heat. Add the onion and cook for about 5 minutes, until starting to soften. Add the garlic and lime leaves and cook for about 2 minutes more, until aromatic. Add the green curry paste and cook for about 3 minutes, stirring often, until lightly colored and aromatic. Stir in the chicken to coat it in the curry paste; cook, stirring, for 5 minutes. Add the coconut milk and bring to a simmer.

Add the bell peppers, asparagus, and green beans, return to a simmer, then reduce the heat and simmer for about 5 minutes, until the vegetables start to soften. Add the bok choy and cook for another 3 minutes, or until all the vegetables are softened and the chicken is cooked through. Set a strainer atop a blender and strain the curry sauce from the pan into the blender, returning the vegetables to the pan. Add the spinach to the blender and blend until smooth and bright green in color. Pour the blended spinach into the pan and add the fish sauce and coconut sugar, if using. Taste and add more fish sauce if needed. Serve immediately, over steamed brown rice if you like.

Do a sweep of your cupboards from time to time. Old Spice only works as an aftershave!

PREP TIME	COOK TIME	SERVES	SMARTPOINTS	CALORIES
20 MINUTES	25 MINUTES	6	6 PER SERVING	217 PER SERVING

Garlic

Whether it's powdered, granulated, raw, blanched, roasted, dehydrated, sautéed, or mashed with salt and made into a paste, garlic is a must. The only thing I don't put it in is dessert.

Black pepper

People take black pepper for granted. But in my kitchen it's an MVP! I grind it over everything from scrambled eggs to cauliflower mashed potatoes. Warning: That pre-ground powdery stuff is like adding a dusting of dust.

Chipotle Peppers

With both smoky and spicy notes, these peppers bring a wallop of flavor to marinades, sauces, and stews.

Truffle Zest

Truffles are the ultimate posh spice. But Truffle Zest only tastes expensive. I've been known to keep it in my bag when I go out to eat.

Celery Seeds

I don't know why celery seeds don't get more play. They add a nice twist to all kinds of salads, smothered chicken, even a Bloody Mary.

OLO
CHIPOTLE PASTE
CONCENTRATED HEAT WITH A DELICATE SMOKY FLAVOR

Vanilla

To smell vanilla fresh from the pod is to never want to exhale—it's a fragrant spice with a rich finish. I like adding it to water with ginger and mint for a no-calorie cocktail.

Basil

Where to begin? First of all, basil is a tomato's best friend! I keep a basil plant in the kitchen and sometimes I just like to cup it in my hands and breathe in the scent of summer.

Crushed red chile flakes

I've never met a chile I didn't like! And here's a bonus: Red chile flakes keep me from adding extra salt. Just don't rub your eyes with fingers that have recently added a pinch of it to something.

Lemon

Almost anything that's delicious without a touch of lemon (salad dressing, popcorn, veggies, fish) will be even more delicious with a touch of lemon!

Ginger

Ginger is pure personality. It's soulful, healing, exotic, and spicy. I use it to flavor water, tea, and almost all of my Asian and Indian dishes.

A HEALTHY INDULGENCE

I adore a pretty table. You can feel the love in the details.

AT MY HOUSE EVERY MEAL IS A CELEBRATION.

I use cloth napkins and good dishes even on the rare occasions when I'm by myself, and if something gets chipped or spilled on—well, I consider a few scuffs and spots the signs of a life that's actually being lived. A home full of kids and dogs, friends and neighbors, is a thing to be treasured. What could be more meaningful than breaking bread with people who make your heart sing?

Breakfast with a few of the grown-up girls from my leadership academy in South Africa.

Enjoying a laugh at the dinner table with Sidney Poitier.

Celebrating at Maya Angelou's 70th birthday dinner.

To me, happiness is the chorus of "oohs" and "aahs" that never fails to follow everyone's first taste of the truffle tortellini.

It's the way Stedman lights up when the tomato and white cheddar pie is sliced. It's holding the platter while Gayle helps herself to a barbecued chicken thigh and offers the wings to her kids, Will and Kirby.

It's the girls from my South African leadership academy asking for seconds on the crab cakes. It's raising your glass to somebody accomplishing something amazing—even if the something amazing is just getting through a crazy week. It's knowing that my sweet pup, Sadie, is standing by under the table, on the off chance she can be of service to anyone who needs help finishing their turkey burger.

It's bad jokes and good stories, and taste this and try that, and should we open another bottle?

It's catching up with your nearest and dearest over food that genuinely delights—that is the ultimate luxury!

I live in a world that happens to include a lot of meticulously planned extravaganzas; I've even thrown a few myself. But the best get-togethers always turn out to be the spontaneous kind, when you call a couple of neighbors and say, "Come on over, we're making breakfast!"

I've shared unforgettable meals with people in a tin shack near Soweto, and in my own home, and I can tell you that luscious food doesn't need to be fancy and neither do the people who are eating it.

The only thing I want my guests to do is show up hungry and leave happy, feeling just a little more connected to each other when it's all said and done.

You see, part of what makes a great meal great is the shared experience. Pasta cacio e pepe (see page 155) is always better enjoyed with your favorite bottle of wine and cool conversation.

Maya Angelou was the master of gathering people from all walks of life and feeding them magnificently. She understood that food creates connection and that every once in a while—if the stars align and the chemistry crackles—acquaintances can become old friends.

I've adopted Maya's way as my own. On any given day, at least four or five "daughters" from my South African leadership academy are at my kitchen table along with whoever else is around. That's what we

Even after all these years, Stedman Graham is still my very favorite face to see every morning over breakfast and the paper.

do. We come together, we say grace, we talk about whatever's going on in the world and in our lives, and we eat well.

For me, today, eating well involves tracking my points and finding creative ways to trim calories. But now that I've finally internalized the rules of clean eating, I let myself break those rules! I don't do it often, and I never do it mindlessly; the goal is to make my indulgences intentional. I aim for deliberate. I plan for decadence.

If the idea of intentional indulgence strikes a chord with you, I hope you'll consider this chapter permission to cut loose, because these recipes come straight from my greatest hits list. If you want a super satisfying, comforting dinner, I highly recommend those chicken pot pies. And while you're at it, treat yourself to the fettuccine bolognese. (There's a reason it's a dish I love to serve guests!)

But here's my advice: Make these dishes special. Share them with someone you cherish. Be sure to savor—really savor—every single bite. Stop yourself from eating past the point of comfort. And do not, under any circumstance, allow yourself even a second of regret.

I've been making this dish since my first apartment kitchen at age 22 and have refined it over the years.

PASTA PRIMAVERA

This is my go-to pasta dish, only now I make it with a lot less pasta and a lot more veggies. The light sauce is so delicious, you won't miss a thing.

INGREDIENTS:

2 tablespoons sea salt, plus more to taste

3 medium carrots, finely chopped

1 medium zucchini, cut into ½-inch cubes

1 cup tiny broccoli florets

8 ounces pasta, such as Montebello Strozzapreti pasta, or the shape of your choice

1 tablespoon extra virgin olive oil

1 medium shallot, minced

3 cloves garlic, minced

6 cremini mushrooms, stems removed and very thinly sliced

1 (14-ounce) can diced tomatoes with juices

1 teaspoon red pepper flakes

1 small yellow bell pepper, cored, seeded, and finely diced

2 tablespoons grated Parmesan cheese

Freshly ground black pepper

Garnishes

¼ cup fresh basil leaves cut into chiffonade

3 tablespoons toasted pine nuts

DIRECTIONS:

Fill a large bowl with ice and water to make an ice-water bath. Bring a large pot of water to a boil and add the salt. Add the carrots, zucchini, and broccoli and cook for about 3 minutes, until crisp tender. Scoop the vegetables out (don't drain the water) using a slotted spoon and transfer to the ice-water bath to cool completely, then drain.

Return the water to a boil, add the pasta, and cook until al dente according to the package directions. Drain.

While the pasta is cooking, heat the oil in a large nonstick skillet over medium heat. Add the shallot and garlic and cook for 2 minutes, or until softened and aromatic. Add the mushrooms and cook for about 5 minutes, until softened, adding a tiny bit of water if they start to stick. Add the tomatoes and juices and red pepper flakes and cook for 10 minutes. Add the blanched carrots, zucchini, and broccoli and the pasta and stir to fully coat them in the tomatoes; cook just until everything is heated through. Remove from the heat, stir in the bell pepper and Parmesan, and season with salt and pepper. Divide among bowls and top with the basil and pine nuts.

PREP TIME	COOK TIME	SERVES	SMARTPOINTS	CALORIES
30 MINUTES	20 MINUTES	6	6 PER SERVING	248 PER SERVING

FETTUCCINE BOLOGNESE WITH PEAS

I love fettuccine and I love peas, so I figured that merging the two could only be really good—and it is!
The peas add a burst of sweetness that cuts through the richness of the sauce.

INGREDIENTS:

1 tablespoon extra virgin olive oil

1 pound ground turkey

½ medium yellow onion, finely chopped

2 medium carrots, finely chopped

3 cloves garlic, finely chopped

1 teaspoon salt, or to taste

½ cup white wine

2 cups whole canned fire-roasted tomatoes, with juices

½ teaspoon red pepper flakes

1 cup Great Chicken Stock (page 42), plus more if needed

2 sprigs fresh thyme

2 tablespoons heavy cream

1 cup fresh or thawed frozen peas

8 ounces cooked fettuccine noodles

¼ cup finely grated Parmesan cheese

DIRECTIONS:

In a large skillet, heat the oil over medium-high heat. Add the ground turkey and cook, breaking the meat up with a wooden spoon, for about 10 minutes, until cooked through and browned. Drain any excess fat from pan. Add the onion, carrots, garlic, and salt and cook, stirring often, for about 8 minutes, until softened. Pour in the wine and cook, stirring often, for about 2 minutes, until mostly evaporated. Crush the tomatoes into the pan, adding their juices as well, and add the red pepper flakes. Bring to a simmer, then lower the heat and simmer for 10 minutes. Add the chicken stock and thyme sprigs, return to a simmer, and simmer for 30 minutes, or until the sauce is nice and thick. Stir in the cream and peas and cook just until the peas are cooked through. Turn off the heat, remove the thyme sprigs, and toss the sauce with the fettuccine. Sprinkle with the Parmesan, spoon into bowls, and serve.

PREP TIME	COOK TIME	SERVES	SMARTPOINTS	CALORIES
15 MINUTES	1 HOUR	6	8 PER SERVING	306 PER SERVING

Save a few points by using turkey instead of beef. The sauce is so tasty you won't notice the difference.

PASTA CACIO E PEPE

RECIPE INSPIRED BY FEDERICO BALESTRA

I first tasted this dish at an Umbrian castle after a truffle hunt. It's heavenly even without the shaved truffles on top. Try Truffle Zest or truffle salt for a less expensive option. Using store-bought dried pasta, this dish is as simple to make as it is delicious to eat.

INGREDIENTS:

12 ounces dry spaghetti

Sea salt

1 cup grated Pecorino Romano cheese, or as needed

Fresh black summer or winter truffle, grated on a Microplane, or Sabatino Truffle Zest

2 teaspoons freshly ground black pepper, or to taste

If you haven't discovered Truffle Zest yet—do!

DIRECTIONS:

Bring a tall saucepan of water to a boil over high heat and season heavily with salt. Add the pasta and cook until al dente according to the package instructions. Set a pasta strainer into a separate large saucepan. Pour the pasta into the strainer, reserving the pasta cooking water in the pan below. Remove the strainer with the pasta inside and ladle out 1/2 cup of the hot pasta liquid into a heatproof container. Create a bain-marie by placing a large heatproof bowl over the saucepan with the hot pasta water. Transfer the drained pasta into the bowl, gradually add the cheese and hot pasta cooking water and, using two large spoons or forks, toss the pasta vigorously until you have a creamy consistency. If the sauce is too watery, add more cheese; if the sauce is too dry, add more pasta water. Top with a sprinkle of grated truffle, a little salt, and the pepper, spoon into bowls, and serve.

PREP TIME	COOK TIME	SERVES	SmartPoints	CALORIES
7 MINUTES	15 MINUTES	6	8 PER SERVING	268 PER SERVING

SPRING PEA MEZZELUNE (HALF-MOONS) WITH TOMATO BRODO

Anything with spring peas in it has my vote! *Brodo* is Italian for broth,
and this version adds a light tomato flavor to the dish.

INGREDIENTS:

Kale Juice

4 large kale leaves

1 tablespoon water

Kale Pasta

2 2/3 cups "00" flour

2 teaspoons sea salt

1 large egg

12 large egg yolks

1 tablespoon kale juice

Semolina flour, as needed

Pea Filling

4 1/2 cups fresh or frozen and
thawed peas

Zest of 4 lemons

Sea salt

Tomato Brodo

4 large heirloom tomatoes
(or any other ripe tomatoes
you have on hand), cut into
chunks

Sea salt and cracked black
pepper

DIRECTIONS:

To make the kale juice: Combine kale and water in a high-speed blender
and blend until the leaves are completely broken down, adding a tiny bit
more water if needed to fully blend. Scrape the mixture into a fine-mesh
strainer set over a bowl and press the kale liquid through. Discard the
solids, keeping the kale juice. Or alternatively, pass the kale leaves through
a juicer.

To make the pasta dough: In a food processor fitted with the blade
attachment, combine the "00" flour and salt and pulse to combine. Add the
egg, egg yolks, and kale juice and continue to pulse until the mixture is sandy
in texture. Empty the dough from the food processor onto a work surface and
knead until it becomes smooth, about 5 minutes, dusting the surface with
flour as necessary to prevent sticking. Wrap the dough in plastic wrap and set
aside to rest at room temperature for 30 minutes to 1 hour.

To make the pea filling: In a blender, combine the peas and lemon zest and
blend until smooth, scraping the sides of the machine as needed. Season with
salt and spoon the puree into a pastry bag fitted with a 1/2-inch open tip.

To make the tomato brodo: Place the tomatoes in a blender and blend
until smooth. Pour the puree into a small saucepan, place over medium-
high heat, bring to a boil, and cook at a boil for about 5 minutes, until the
color of the liquid deepens and the solids and juices separate a little. Line a
piece of cheesecloth over a fine-mesh strainer set over a bowl and pour the
pureed tomatoes through it, pressing on the solids to get out all the liquid.
Discard the tomato solids and season with salt and pepper. Reheat the
brodo just before serving.

To form and cook the pasta dough: Secure a pasta roller to a work
surface and dust the work surface with semolina flour. Divide the pasta
dough into 4 pieces, keeping the remaining pieces wrapped in plastic at
room temperature. Or you can freeze the dough, tightly wrapped in plastic
and placed in a freezer bag, for up to 1 month. Thaw the dough at room

PREP TIME	COOK TIME	SERVES	SMARTPOINTS	CALORIES
1 HOUR	1 HOUR		9 PER SERVING	321 PER SERVING

You don't have to make the mezzelune all at once—they can be filled and frozen for later.

temperature overnight. (It is not recommended to refrigerate fresh pasta dough.) Dust the dough lightly with flour and, using your hands, flatten it into a ¼-inch-thick rectangle shape; feel free to add additional flour at any time while you're rolling to keep the dough from sticking.

Set the pasta roller to 1 (the thickest setting) and run the pasta through. Next, set the machine to 2 and run the dough through again. Then set the machine to 3 and work your way progressively through each setting, ending with 6 or 7. You will have a long, 6-inch-wide strip of pasta dough on your work surface.

To form the half-moons: Using a sharp cookie or biscuit cutter, punch out 3-inch rounds; you should have about 36 pieces. Dust the pieces lightly with semolina flour, then cover with a clean, damp kitchen towel to keep them from drying out. Sprinkle a baking sheet with semolina flour.

Working in batches, fill 6 pasta rounds at a time: Lay pasta flat on a work surface and place about a teaspoon of pea filling in the center of each round. Brush the outer edge lightly with water and fold over to make a half-moon, pressing the joined edge flat to seal. Press the dough flat between the portions of filling. Transfer to a baking sheet. Continue until you have run out of filling or dough. Cover baking sheet with plastic wrap.

Bring a large pot of salted water to a boil. To avoid overcrowding the cooking pot, cook the pasta in two separate batches. Add half of the mezzelune and stir so that they don't stick to the bottom of the pan or each other. Cook for 4 to 5 minutes, until they float to the top. If there are air pockets in the mezzelune, they may rise to the top but not necessarily be done. Remove one mezzelune with a slotted spoon and test for doneness. When the pasta is done, remove it from the water using a slotted spoon and set it into a bowl. Begin cooking the second batch of pasta in the same manner while you plate the first batch. Divide the pasta among shallow bowls, pour ¼ cup of the hot brodo over the pasta, season with salt and pepper, and serve.

PENNE PASTA WITH CHICKEN, SUN-DRIED TOMATOES, AND BASIL

This pasta is a crowd-pleaser. In the early days at Harpo Studios, we had daily production staff meetings. The whole team would get together in my office and eat lunch. There was a lot shared over bowls of this pasta. One year at the farm, we had a garden with an abundance of basil—that's how this recipe came to be.

INGREDIENTS:

4 boneless, skinless chicken thighs (about 12 ounces)

1 teaspoon Italian seasoning

Salt and freshly ground black pepper

3 tablespoons extra virgin olive oil

4 garlic cloves, sliced

8 ounces penne pasta, cooked to al dente

½ medium yellow bell pepper, cored, seeded, and cut into ¼-inch cubes

½ cup sun-dried tomatoes, soaked in hot water to cover for 30 minutes, drained, and cut into thin strips

¼ cup pitted kalamata olives, cut in half

3 tablespoons drained capers

¼ cup crumbled feta cheese

2 tablespoons fresh lemon juice, or to taste

½ teaspoon grated lemon zest

½ cup chopped fresh basil

3 tablespoons pine nuts, toasted

DIRECTIONS:

Sprinkle the Italian seasoning over the chicken and season with salt and pepper on both sides. Heat 2 tablespoons of the oil in a large skillet over medium-high heat. Add the garlic and cook for 1 minute, or until it just starts to color. Add the chicken to the pan, cover, and cook for about 6 minutes on each side, until cooked through, reserving the juices in the pan to reheat the pasta. Remove the chicken from the pan to a plate and cool for a couple of minutes.

While the chicken is cooling, whisk ½ cup water into the drippings left in the pan from cooking the chicken, bring to a simmer over medium heat, and simmer for about 5 minutes, until slightly thickened. Add the pasta and cook, stirring, until warmed through.

Slice the chicken into strips. In a large bowl, combine the chicken, pasta, bell pepper, sun-dried tomatoes, olives, capers, and cheese. In a small bowl, whisk together the lemon juice, lemon zest, and the remaining 1 tablespoon oil. Pour it over the pasta and mix to coat all the ingredients. Stir in the basil. Taste and add more salt, pepper, and/or lemon juice if needed. Spoon into bowls and serve topped with the pine nuts.

PREP TIME	COOK TIME	SERVES	SMARTPOINTS	CALORIES
20 MINUTES	**30** MINUTES	**6**	**9** PER SERVING	**324** PER SERVING

The dish can also be served cold with a large green salad.

TURKEY MEATLOAF

Turkey is fewer points than regular beef meatloaf and I promise, once you try this, it will become your new standard meatloaf.

INGREDIENTS:

Meatloaf

2 teaspoons extra virgin olive oil

1 carrot, finely diced

½ medium yellow onion, finely diced

1 rib celery, finely diced

3 cloves garlic, grated on a Microplane

½ teaspoon kosher salt

¼ teaspoon freshly ground black pepper

1 pound ground dark meat turkey

1 small egg, beaten

¼ cup Great Chicken Stock (page 42)

¼ cup panko breadcrumbs

1 teaspoon finely chopped fresh flat-leaf parsley

1 teaspoon dried thyme

1 teaspoon blackening spice

Chipotle Ketchup Glaze

⅓ cup ketchup

1 teaspoon ground cumin

½ teaspoon Worcestershire sauce

1 teaspoon chipotle paste

1 teaspoon agave nectar

¼ teaspoon freshly ground black pepper

½ teaspoon kosher salt

DIRECTIONS:

Preheat the oven to 350°F and line an 8 x 12–inch baking sheet with parchment paper.

Heat the oil in a large skillet over medium-low heat. Add the carrot, onion, and celery and cook until softened but not colored, about 5 minutes. Add the garlic and cook for 1 minute, or until aromatic. Stir in the salt and pepper, transfer to a plate, and cool completely.

In a large bowl, combine the turkey and egg, mixing them together using a large spoon or your hands. Stir in the cooked vegetables, the chicken stock, breadcrumbs, parsley, thyme, and blackening spice. Scrape the mixture into a mound onto the baking sheet and shape it into an 8 x 3–inch freeform loaf. Place in the oven and bake for 30 to 35 minutes, until the meatloaf reaches an internal temperature of 165°F when tested with an instant-read thermometer. Remove from the oven and set aside to rest while you make the glaze.

Turn the broiler to low.

In a small saucepan, whisk together all of the glaze ingredients, place over medium heat, and bring just to a boil, whisking continuously to prevent sticking.

Pour the glaze over the top of the meatloaf and use a spatula to spread it in a thick, even layer. Place the meatloaf in the broiler and broil until the glaze begins to bubble and caramelize. Remove the meatloaf from the broiler, let it sit for 5 minutes, then slice and serve.

PREP TIME	COOK TIME	SERVES	SMARTPOINTS	CALORIES
30 MINUTES	30–35 MINUTES	4	6 PER SERVING	258 PER SERVING

TURKEY BURGERS

My friend Gayle is always on a quest for the all-time best burger, and this turkey version is at the top of her list.

INGREDIENTS:

1 ½ pounds ground turkey (dark meat)

½ red apple, cored and roughly chopped

2 tablespoons mango chutney

1 scallion, white and green parts roughly chopped

2 cloves garlic, grated on a Microplane

¼ cup fresh cilantro leaves

1 tablespoon soy sauce

½ teaspoon curry powder

½ teaspoon ground chipotle

1 teaspoon sea salt

Grapeseed or coconut oil cooking spray

Your choice of condiments

4 pretzel buns, such as Röckenwagner brand

DIRECTIONS:

Place the turkey in a large bowl, cover with a dish towel, and let come to room temperature while you prep the rest of the ingredients.

In a food processor, combine the apple, mango chutney, scallion, garlic, cilantro, soy sauce, curry powder, chipotle, and salt and process until smooth. Add the mixture to the turkey and mix thoroughly to combine. Divide the mixture into four equal portions and form each into a loose ball. Pat lightly to flatten the meat into burgers about ¾ inch thick.

Heat a large, heavy skillet, preferably cast-iron, over medium-high heat. Spray with a thin layer of oil and add the burgers. Cook until nicely browned on the bottom, 4 to 5 minutes, then flip the burgers, reduce the heat to medium-low, cover the pan, and cook for about 6 minutes, until browned on the bottom and cooked through. Remove from the pan and serve.

While the burgers are cooking, place the split pretzel buns on the grill cut side down to toast them (or toast them in a toaster). Remove the buns from the grill, sandwich the burgers into the buns, and add your choice of condiments.

PREP TIME	COOK TIME	SERVES	SmartPoints	CALORIES
10 MINUTES	10 MINUTES	4	5 PER SERVING	264 PER SERVING (DOES NOT INCLUDE BUNS OR CONDIMENTS)

CRAB CAKES

I lived in Baltimore for eight years, where, Hon, they know a thing or two
about crab cakes. These are nearly as good as what you get there.

INGREDIENTS:

1 large egg

2 tablespoons mayonnaise

1 clove garlic, grated on a Microplane

1 tablespoon fresh lemon juice

1 teaspoon sweet paprika, plus more for dusting

1 teaspoon Old Bay Seasoning

¾ teaspoon salt

2 teaspoons minced fresh parsley

1 teaspoon prepared yellow mustard

1 pound lump crab meat, drained of
any excess liquid

2 slices white bread (day-old or semi-stale is
fine), crusts removed and finely crumbled, or
½ cup panko breadcrumbs

Extra virgin olive oil cooking spray

DIRECTIONS:

In a large bowl, beat the egg. Whisk in the
mayonnaise, garlic, lemon juice, paprika, Old Bay,
salt, parsley, and mustard. Add the crab and mix to
combine, then mix in the crumbled bread. Shape
the mixture into 8 equal-size rounds and place on
a broiler pan. Generously spray with cooking spray
and dust with a little paprika. Place in the broiler
and broil for 5 to 8 minutes, until golden brown on
top. Remove from the broiler and serve immediately.

PREP TIME	COOK TIME	SERVES	SmartPoints	CALORIES
15	5–8	8	2	99
MINUTES	MINUTES		PER SERVING	PER SERVING

Pssst... the secret is the lump crab!

SIPPING PRETTY

BRILLIANT THINKING ALL ABOUT DRINKING

There are very few drinks that aren't high on the point scale—especially when vodka is added at 2 points per ounce. But there's nothing I enjoy more than sitting on the porch and watching the sunset over cocktails with friends. My house manager, Eddie, has mastered the art of concocting fun, interesting combinations of whatever fresh fruits, vegetables, and herbs are available. Some are crisp and refreshing, some are smoking with flavor, others are just smoking hot—the guy loves a jalapeño! Whatever suits your sipping style, take a little time to see the sun set.

Sexy Green Smoothie

1 cup cold water

1 medium cucumber, peeled, seeded, and chopped

1 ripe banana, broken into pieces

½ organic Granny Smith apple, cored, seeded, and chopped

½ thumb-size piece ginger, peeled

¾ cup chopped fresh kale leaves

2 cups fresh spinach leaves

4 fresh mint leaves

4 fresh basil leaves

2 ounces protein powder, such as PlantFusion Complete Plant Protein (unflavored)

1 cup ice cubes

Pour the cold water into a blender. Add the cucumber, banana, apple, and ginger and blend until liquefied. Add the kale, spinach, mint, and basil a handful at a time, blending in batches until it is all blended in. Add the protein powder and ice cubes and blend until the ice cubes are crushed and the smoothie is smooth.

SERVES 2

5 SMARTPOINTS PER SERVING

Cleansing Lemonade/Cold Buster

6 fresh basil leaves, roughly torn

Juice of 4 lemons

Juice of 1 medium grapefruit

2 tablespoons apple cider vinegar

Pinch of ground cayenne

Place the basil in a sturdy glass, add a few small ice cubes, and muddle the basil with the ice. Add the lemon juice, grapefruit juice, vinegar, and cayenne. Stir, leave for a few minutes for the basil to infuse into the juice, and serve.

SERVES 4-5 | 2 SMARTPOINTS PER 8 OZ. SERVING

T8 Juice

6 super-ripe tomatoes, preferably organic

½ beet, peeled and roughly chopped

1 small bunch kale

1 small bunch spinach

4 ribs celery, including leaves

3 medium cucumbers, cut into chunks

3 scallions, ends trimmed

3 cloves garlic, peeled

½ cup fresh basil leaves

½ cup fresh parsley leaves

2 orange bell peppers, cored and cut into chunks

Juice of 2 lemons

½ teaspoon freshly ground black pepper, or to taste

½ teaspoon ground cayenne, or to taste

Large pinch of sea salt

Pass the tomatoes, beet, kale, spinach, celery, cucumbers, scallions, garlic, basil, parsley, and bell peppers through a juicer. Pour into a pitcher or jar, add the lemon juice, black pepper, cayenne, and salt, and serve, over ice if you like.

SERVES 4-5
4 SmartPoints
PER 8 oz. SERVING

This is the ultimate juice to make for a busy week. It's delicious, an amazing source of energy, and keeps well in the refrigerator for up to 4 days. Also makes one mean Bloody Mary!

Maui in December

Smoked and Infused Pineapple

1 large fresh pineapple

2 stalks fresh lemongrass, root ends trimmed and outer leaves reserved for garnish

1 (750-ml) bottle vodka

3 fresh mint leaves

1 chamomile tea bag

MAKES 2 COCKTAILS PLUS EXTRA INFUSED VODKA FOR PLENTY MORE
8 SmartPoints PER SERVING

Cocktails

2 thumbnail-size slices fresh peeled ginger

Ice cubes

½ cup smoked pineapple and lemongrass infused vodka (see left)

½ cup fresh pineapple juice (see left)

¼ cup cold chamomile tea (see left)

1 tablespoon fresh lemon juice

Cut off the top and bottom and trim the pineapple with a serrated knife. Cut it into quarters and slice out the core from each quarter. Place two quarters in the blender, blend until smooth, then strain the liquid through a fine-mesh sieve into a bowl. Transfer to a bottle or other nonreactive container, and refrigerate.

Place the remaining pineapple and lemongrass on a barbecue or stovetop grill pan at medium high, cover, and smoke for 4–5 minutes on each side. Then put the smoked pineapple and lemongrass in a large canning jar with the vodka and mint. Cover the jar and refrigerate for 8 hours or overnight.

Boil water and make the tea in a large canning jar. Cool to room temperature, then cover and refrigerate for at least 8 hours or overnight.

To make the cocktails, muddle the ginger in a shaker and fill it with ice cubes. Add ½ cup infused vodka, pineapple juice, ¼ tea, and ½ cup lemon juice. Shake and strain into chilled martini glasses. Garnish with lemongrass leaves and serve.

Picante Margarita!

SERVES 1
8 SmartPoints
PER SERVING

1–2 jalapeño slices

4 ounces chopped green apples

2 fresh mint leaves

3 fresh basil leaves

3 oz fresh lime juice

2 tablespoons organic simple syrup (see syrup recipe at right)

2 ounces tequila blanco (silver)

To make syrup: Bring 1 cup organic sugarcane and 1 cup water to boil in a saucepan, stirring to dissolve sugar. Let simple syrup cool.

To make margarita: Muddle jalapeño, apples, mint, and basil in a cocktail shaker. Add the lime juice, syrup, tequila. Fill shaker with ice, shake about 30 seconds. Strain into a rocks glass filled with ice and garnish with a jalapeño slice.

BARBECUE CHICKEN

Is there anyone who doesn't love a good barbecued chicken?
I like it hot off the grill or straight from the fridge.

INGREDIENTS:

Brine

1 quart water

¼ cup honey

¼ cup salt

1 tablespoon pickling spice

1 tablespoon chili powder

1 tablespoon granulated garlic

1 tablespoon ground cumin

1 teaspoon ground chipotle chile

4 pounds bone-in mixed chicken legs, thighs, and breast

1 medium orange, cut into 6 pieces

Barbecue Sauce

MAKES ABOUT 4 CUPS

1 tablespoon extra virgin olive oil

1 medium onion, finely chopped

1 medium red bell pepper, cored, seeded, and finely chopped

3 cloves garlic, crushed through a garlic press

1 cup Dijon-style mustard

½ cup ketchup

1 cup orange juice

1 cup apple juice

1 cup light soy sauce

1 cup apple cider vinegar

2 teaspoons ground chipotle chile

2 teaspoons sea salt

Use the leftover sauce to baste or marinade anything you plan on grilling. Keeps for up to a week.

DIRECTIONS:

To make the brine: Combine all the brine ingredients in a medium saucepan and bring to a boil over high heat. Boil, stirring often, until the salt has dissolved, about 5 minutes. Do not let the liquid reduce or the brine will become too salty. Remove from the heat and cool completely. Put the chicken and the orange in a large zip-top bag, set the bag in a container, add the brine, secure the bag, and refrigerate for 2 to 4 hours.

To make the barbecue sauce: Heat the oil in a large saucepan over medium heat. Add the onion and cook until well browned, about 10 minutes. Add the bell pepper and cook until softened, about 5 minutes. Add the garlic and cook, stirring, for 1 minute. Add the remaining ingredients, bring to a simmer, then reduce the heat to medium and cook uncovered for about 45 minutes, until it starts to thicken. Use an immersion blender to blend the sauce directly in the pan, then continue to cook until the sauce thickly coats the back of a spoon, about 15 minutes more.

To cook the chicken on an outdoor grill: Heat a grill to a medium heat and oil the grates. Remove the chicken from the brine, pat it dry with paper towels, and place it on the grill. Grill for 5 to 10 minutes on each side, until the chicken begins to release from the grill and the skin starts to crisp. Turn and cook to grill-sear all sides, then move the chicken to a cooler portion of the grill and baste it with the barbecue sauce. Leave until the sauce becomes tacky and an instant-read thermometer reads 160°F when inserted in the thickest part of the meat. Remove the chicken from the grill and let rest for 5 to 10 minutes before serving.

To cook the chicken in the oven: Preheat the oven to 450°F. Line a baking sheet with aluminum foil and set a wire rack on top of the sheet. Remove the chicken from the brine, pat it dry with paper towels, and place it on the rack with a little space between each piece. Place the chicken in the oven and roast for 10 minutes, or until the skin starts to crisp. Baste the chicken with barbecue sauce and roast for another 30 to 40 minutes, basting every 10 minutes or so, until the barbecue sauce nicely coats the chicken and the chicken is well browned all over. Remove the chicken from the oven and let rest for 5 to 10 minutes before serving.

PREP TIME	COOK TIME	SERVES	SMARTPOINTS	CALORIES
20	1	8	11	385
MINUTES (PLUS 2–4 HRS BRINING)	HOUR		PER SERVING	PER SERVING

CHICKEN POTPIE

RECIPE INSPIRED BY CHEF WOLFGANG PUCK AND CHEF MATT BENCIVENGA

Does anything say comfort like a chicken potpie? I don't think so.
It's the cashmere blanket of dinners, perfect for a cool evening at home.

INGREDIENTS:

Crust

1 ¾ cups gluten-free pie crust mix, such as Bob's Red Mill, plus more for rolling the dough

⅛ teaspoon Sabatino Truffle Zest

6 tablespoons cold unsalted butter or vegetable shortening, cut into ½-inch cubes

3 tablespoons ice water

1 large egg, beaten

Sauce

Extra virgin olive oil cooking spray

1 ½ cups finely diced onion

¾ cup finely diced carrot

¼ cup finely diced celery

1 teaspoon minced fresh thyme

Sea salt

1 quart Great Chicken Stock (page 42)

½ teaspoon Sabatino Truffle Zest

Freshly ground white pepper

Filling

Extra virgin olive oil cooking spray

1 ¼ pounds boneless, skinless chicken breasts, cut into ¾-inch pieces

1 small yellow onion, chopped

2 medium carrots, cut into ½-inch cubes

1 rib celery, cut into ½-inch cubes

4 ounces cremini mushrooms, diced

⅔ cup frozen petite peas, thawed

DIRECTIONS:

To make the crust: Combine the pie crust mix and Truffle Zest in a food processor fitted with the blade attachment and pulse to combine. Add the butter and pulse 10 times, or until the butter breaks into pea-size pieces. Transfer the mixture into a large bowl and gradually add the ice water, mixing the dough with your hands until it just comes together. Slightly flatten the dough into a ball, wrap in plastic wrap, and refrigerate for at least 1 hour or up to 24 hours.

To make the sauce: Preheat oven to 400°F and coat a baking sheet with cooking spray.

In a medium bowl, toss together the onions, carrot, celery, and thyme. Spread the vegetables onto the baking sheet, spray them lightly with cooking spray, and season with salt. Place the sheet in the oven and roast for 20 minutes, or until well browned, stirring a few times to ensure even browning.

While the vegetables are roasting, pour the chicken stock into a medium saucepan. Place over medium-high heat, bring to a boil, and boil until it reduces by half, about 8 to 10 minutes. Add the vegetables to the stock and cook for about 5 minutes, until they are completely softened. Transfer the stock and vegetables to the blender, add the Truffle Zest, and blend until smooth. Season with salt and pepper. Place a spoon in the sauce to check that the sauce coats the spoon. If the sauce isn't thick enough, pour it into a medium saucepan and cook over low heat, stirring with a wooden spoon, until it reaches the correct consistency.

PREP TIME	COOK TIME	SERVES	SmartPoints	CALORIES
20 MINUTES	**30** MINUTES	**5**	**16** PER SERVING	**494** PER SERVING

To make the filling: Coat a large cast-iron skillet with cooking spray and heat over medium-high heat. Add the chicken and cook until it is lightly browned, about 5 minutes. Transfer the chicken to a large bowl. Add a little more cooking spray, then add the onions to the pan and cook until it begins to brown, about 5 minutes, then add the carrots and celery and cook for 3 to 4 minutes, until they begin to soften. Add the mushrooms and cook for an additional 2 to 3 minutes, until all the vegetables are softened, then add them to the bowl with the chicken. Stir in the peas. Pour the sauce over the chicken and vegetable mixture and stir to combine well.

To assemble and bake the potpies: Coat 5 eight-ounce ramekins with cooking spray. Using a ladle, portion 1 cup of the filling mixture into each ramekin. Cool completely, then transfer the ramekins to the refrigerator while you roll out the crust.

Preheat the oven to 375°F.

Lightly dust a work surface with gluten-free flour. Roll the dough out $1/8$ inch thick and brush free any excess flour. Cut out five 4-inch disks that slightly overlap the top of the ramekins. Cut a small hole in the center of the disks, place one dough disk on top of each ramekin, and gently press the top sides to adhere to the edge of the dish. Place the potpies onto a parchment paper–lined baking sheet and lightly brush the dough tops with the beaten egg. Bake for 30 minutes, or until the tops are golden brown and the filling is hot. Remove from the oven and serve immediately.

This dish is worth every second it takes to prepare.

TOMATO AND WHITE CHEDDAR PIE

RECIPE FROM CHEF ART SMITH

A Southern classic I grew up eating in Mississippi. We served this to the crew working on this book, and they all said it was the best thing they'd ever tasted.

INGREDIENTS:

Crust

2 ½ cups self-rising flour

2 tablespoons cold unsalted butter, cut into ½-inch cubes

2 tablespoons cold vegetable shortening, cut into ½-inch cubes

¼ cup grated white cheddar cheese

½ cup buttermilk, plus more if needed

Extra virgin olive oil cooking spray

Tomato filling

3 cups baby pear or grape tomatoes, cut in half

1 cup grated white cheddar cheese

2 tablespoons chopped fresh chives

2 tablespoons all-purpose flour

2 tablespoons unsalted butter

1 Vidalia onion, chopped

2 cloves garlic, minced

1 jalapeño chile, seeded and minced

Sea salt and freshly ground black pepper

1 large egg white, beaten with 2 tablespoons water

DIRECTIONS:

To make the crust: In a food processor (or by hand with a pastry blender in a mixing bowl), combine the flour, butter, shortening, and cheese and pulse until the butter and shortening break into pea-size pieces. Gradually add the buttermilk and process until the dough comes together. If the dough is too dry, add more buttermilk, 1 tablespoon at a time, and pulse to combine. You want the dough to be moist enough to form a ball but not wet. Form the dough into a flattened disk, wrap in plastic wrap, and refrigerate for at least 1 hour or up to 24 hours before using.

To make the tomato filling: In a large bowl, combine the tomatoes, cheese, chives, and flour and mix thoroughly with a wooden spoon to combine. Set aside.

Melt the butter in a sauté pan over medium heat. Add the onion, garlic, and chiles and cook until the onions are translucent, about 5 minutes. Remove from the heat and add to the bowl with the tomato mixture. Using a wooden spoon, stir to combine all the ingredients. Season with salt and pepper and set aside to cool to room temperature.

To assemble and bake the pie: Remove the dough from the refrigerator and cut it in half. Coat an 8-inch tart or pie pan with cooking spray. Lightly flour a work surface and roll out one disk of dough into a 10-inch circle. Brush free any excess flour and set the dough into the pan, fitting it snug into the bottom and along the sides. Pour the prepared tomato mixture into the pie dough–lined pan and, using a metal spatula, smooth the top flat.

Lightly flour the work surface again and roll out the second half of dough into a 10-inch circle. Brush free any excess flour. Using a pastry wheel or knife (like the one on page 219), cut out twelve ½-inch strips and lay the strips over the top of the pie in a crisscross manner, creating a basket weave. Gently press the strips of dough against the outer rim, then trim off the excess dough with a paring knife. Brush the top with the egg white mixture and sprinkle lightly with salt and pepper.

Preheat the oven to 400°F and line a baking sheet with parchment paper. Set the pie on the prepared baking sheet and place in the oven. Bake for 10 minutes, then reduce the oven temperature to 375°F and bake for an additional 35 minutes, or until the pie crust is golden brown and bubbling. Place on a cooling rack to cool for 30 minutes before serving, or cool completely and serve at room temperature. The cooled tart will keep, wrapped in plastic wrap, in the refrigerator for up to 3 days.

PREP TIME	COOK TIME	SERVES	SmartPoints	CALORIES
30 MINUTES	55 MINUTES	8	11 PER SERVING	337 PER SERVING

"WHAT I KNOW
FOR SURE IS
THAT WHAT YOU
GIVE COMES
BACK TO YOU."

—OPRAH WINFREY

HOLIDAY TURKEY

I've seen fabulous-looking Thanksgiving birds come to the table all decked out on a silver platter garnished with oranges and pomegranates and looking like a Flemish oil painting hanging at the Met! But when you actually take a bite, it's like eating cardboard. Follow every step here, and I guarantee your turkey will be gorgeous, moist, full of flavor, and totally gobble-up-able.

INGREDIENTS:

1/3 cup black peppercorns

6 bay leaves

3 tablespoons juniper berries

2 large yellow onions, chopped

1 head garlic, cloves peeled and smashed

3 gallons water

2 1/2 cups kosher salt

2 cups red wine vinegar

1/2 bunch fresh thyme

1/2 bunch fresh rosemary

1 (20-pound) organic turkey

DIRECTIONS:

Heat a large saucepan over medium heat. Add the peppercorns, bay leaves, and juniper berries and cook until fragrant, about 3 minutes. Add the onions and garlic and cook for another minute, then add 1 quart of the water and the salt, increase the heat to high, and bring to a boil, stirring to dissolve the salt. Add the remaining water, the vinegar, thyme, and rosemary. Pour the brine into a 5-gallon bucket (or, alternatively, use a brining bag). Place the turkey into the brine breast side down, making sure the cavity gets filled and the bird is fully submerged. Refrigerate for 24 hours.

Preheat the oven to 425°F and adjust an oven rack to the lower middle position.

Remove the turkey from the brine and pat dry with paper towels. Place the turkey breast side up on a wire rack set into a roasting pan. Turn the wings back to stabilize the turkey. Place in the oven with the legs facing the back of the oven. Roast for 20 minutes, then lower the oven temperature to 325°F and continue to roast, basting every 30 minutes, for about 3 1/2 hours, until the thickest part of the turkey thigh reaches 165°F. If any part of the turkey starts to darken in color too much, tent that section with aluminum foil. Remove from the oven, lift the turkey onto a platter, and let rest for 15 minutes before carving.

PREP TIME	COOK TIME	SERVES	SMARTPOINTS	CALORIES
15	4	**16**	8	549
MINUTES	HOURS		PER SERVING	PER SERVING
(PLUS 24 HRS REFRIGERATION)				

CORNBREAD DRESSING WITH TURKEY SAUSAGE, APPLES, AND SAGE

RECIPE FROM CHEF ART SMITH

I eat this only once a year, but suffice it to say, Thanksgiving is not the day I choose to practice portion control—not when it comes to this!

INGREDIENTS:

3 tablespoons extra virgin olive oil

1 pound turkey sausage, casings removed

2 yellow onions, chopped

2 Granny Smith apples, peeled, cored, and chopped

3 ribs celery, chopped

Salt

2 tablespoons chopped fresh sage

3 tablespoons chopped fresh parsley

2 teaspoons fresh thyme leaves

1 loaf cornbread, cut into cubes and left overnight to dry out (about 8 cups)

4 cups cubed soft whole wheat or white bread, left overnight to dry out

3 large eggs, beaten

2 cups Great Chicken Stock (page 42), heated, plus more if needed

Salt and freshly ground black pepper

DIRECTIONS:

Preheat the oven to 375°F and lightly oil an 8 x 10-inch casserole dish.

Heat 1 tablespoon of the oil in a large skillet over medium-high heat. Add the sausage and cook, stirring often, until it loses its pink color, about 5 minutes. Transfer to a large bowl. Add the remaining 2 tablespoons oil to the skillet, add the onions, reduce the heat to medium, and cook for about 5 minutes, until translucent. Add the apples, celery, and ½ teaspoon salt and cook for about 10 minutes, until softened but not broken down or mushy, then add them to the bowl with the sausage. Fold in the sage, parsley, and thyme. Add the dried bread cubes to the bowl and toss to combine. Stir in the eggs and add enough of the chicken stock to moisten the dressing. Season with salt and pepper.

Spread the mixture into the prepared baking dish. If the dish seems dry around the edges, drizzle in some more stock. Cover with foil and bake for about 45 minutes, until lightly browned on top, removing the foil halfway though baking for a crunchy top.

PREP TIME	COOK TIME	SERVES	SMARTPOINTS	CALORIES
20 MINUTES	70 MINUTES	12	7 PER SERVING	254 PER SERVING

Potatoes are high in potassium, and the skin is the most nutritious part.

TWICE-BAKED POTATOES

This always reminds me of the baked potatoes I would get scouring the food court in Maryland, but as twice-baked potatoes go, here's one that's a whole lot healthier!

INGREDIENTS:

2 large baking potatoes, such as russet

Salt

1 cup very small broccoli florets

2 tablespoons reduced-fat sour cream or cottage cheese

4 tablespoons grated cheddar cheese

Kernels from 1 small ear corn (about ½ cup)

2 tablespoons chopped scallions

½ teaspoon freshly ground black pepper

To make this over-the-top delicious I would sprinkle with lots of Truffle Zest.

DIRECTIONS:

Preheat the oven to 400°F.

Scrub the potatoes, then poke them with a fork in a few places. Put them directly on an oven rack and bake for 45 minutes to 1 hour, until a fork pierces a potato without resistance. Remove the potatoes from the oven and increase the oven temperature to 425°F.

Meanwhile, fill a medium saucepan with water, place over high heat, and bring to a boil. Salt the water, then add the broccoli and cook for about 45 seconds, until it is slightly softened but still crisp and bright green. Strain, then rinse with cold water. Pat dry with a paper towel and set aside.

Cut the potatoes in half and scoop out the centers, leaving enough of the flesh to make a nice sturdy base to hold the filling. Put potato skins in a baking dish and put the flesh in a bowl. Mash the potato flesh with a fork or potato masher.

Add the sour cream, 2 tablespoons of the cheese, the corn kernels, scallions, ½ teaspoon salt, and the pepper to the bowl with the potato flesh and gently mix to combine. Spoon the filling into the prepared potato skins and arrange the broccoli florets on top so they stand like little trees. Sprinkle with the remaining 2 tablespoons cheese, place in the oven, and bake for 15 minutes, or until the cheese is melted and bubbly.

Note: The stuffed potatoes may be assembled a day ahead; store covered in the refrigerator. To heat them up, place them on a baking dish and bake for 20 minutes, or until heated through.

PREP TIME	COOK TIME	SERVES	SMARTPOINTS	CALORIES
75 MINUTES	1 HOUR	4	6 PER SERVING	205 PER SERVING

Snack Time

Sometimes a small snack staves off serious hunger. I'm not talking about mindless munching or regular trips to the vending machine; I snack on a controlled portion of something fun and healthy no more than once or twice a day. Here are three favorites to have on hand for a little pick-me-up.

TRUFFLED POTATO CHIPS

The first time I made these and they turned out perfectly, I actually teared up from happiness!

---

3 very fresh medium red bliss potatoes
Extra virgin olive oil cooking spray
Sabatino truffle salt

Preheat the oven to 350°F. Line a 12 x 17-inch baking sheet with a silicone mat or parchment paper and coat it evenly with cooking spray.

Using a mandoline, slice the potatoes $1/16$ inch thick and place them in a large bowl. Rinse the potato slices under cold water and drain. Lay the slices between sheets of paper towel and pat them dry to eliminate excess moisture.

Lay the potato slices onto the baking sheet, placing them close together but without touching. Lightly spray the tops of the potato slices with cooking spray and cover them with a second silicone mat or a sheet of parchment paper. Cover with a second baking sheet to hold the potatoes flat while they are in the oven.

Place the potatoes in the oven and bake for 10 minutes, then check their progress; the chips are done when they turn golden brown and crisp. The chips toward the outside edges of the sheet may be ready before the ones in the middle; simply remove the outer chips with a metal spatula to a cooling rack and season immediately with truffle salt. Cover and return the less done chips to the oven and check them again in 5 minutes. Continue removing batches, immediately placing each batch on the cooling rack and seasoning with truffle salt as it comes out of the oven, until all the chips are golden brown and crisp. Serve immediately.

SERVES 4
3 SMARTPOINTS PER SERVING

Select very fresh potatoes to ensure a crispy chip.

KALE CHIPS

A cautionary kale tale: On the way to an event a
while back, I snacked on a little bag of my homemade
kale chips to keep from being tempted by the hors
d'oeuvres. There I am, smiling away, when someone
pulls me aside and whispers: "I know you'll be
taking a lot of pictures; your teeth are kind of, uh...
green." I thought she meant a flake of kale had gotten
wedged somewhere, so I swished my tongue back
and forth a few times and asked, "Did I get it?" She
averted her eyes and answered, "Um, you should go
to the bathroom." Well, I took one look in the ladies'
room mirror and oh NOOO! It was like my teeth had
decided to celebrate Saint Patrick's Day at a party in
June! My entire mouth was green, which raised the
question, how many people had seen this without
saying a word? All evening I kept going back to the
woman who saved me to say thank you so much!
Thank you SO much! By my third thank you, she
thought I was stalking her. My point: Try the kale
chips, but always do a pre-party mirror check!

---

1 bunch curly or Tuscan kale, washed and
thoroughly dried

Extra virgin olive oil spray

1 teaspoon blackening spice

Fine sea salt

Preheat the oven to 350°F.

Remove the kale stems and tear the kale into
1 ½- to 2-inch pieces. Lay the kale on one or
two baking sheets lined with silicone mats or
parchment paper. Cover the kale with a light
spray of olive oil and lightly dust the chips with
blackening seasoning. Transfer to the oven and
bake for 10 minutes. Check the chips; if a few of
them need a little more time, remove the ones
that are ready and return the sheet or sheets to
the oven for a few more minutes to crisp up the
remaining chips. Season with salt.

SERVES 2

0 SMARTPOINTS PER SERVING

*Look for smaller, younger leaves if
you prefer curly kale. Kale chips are even
more satisfying mixed with other
treats like popcorn (see right).*

TRUFFLE AND
LEMON POPCORN

Say hello to my all-time greatest snack! I find the
best way to eat popcorn is with a classic movie and
a minimum of three dogs snuggled up around me!

---

2 tablespoons grapeseed oil

⅓ cup popcorn kernels

½ teaspoon fine sea salt

¼ teaspoon freshly ground black pepper

½ teaspoon Sabatino Truffle Zest

2 teaspoons fresh lemon juice

Heat the oil in a 3-quart or larger pot over medium-high
heat. Put 3 or 4 kernels in the pot and cover the pot. When
the starter kernels pop, add the rest of the kernels, gently
shaking the pan to set them in an even layer, and put
the lid back on. Remove from the heat for 30 seconds;
this tempers the kernels to allow them to pop at around
the same time. Return the pot to the heat, and once the
kernels begin to pop, between 30 seconds and 1 minute,
gently move the pot back and forth over the burner. Once
the popcorn slows to several seconds between pops,
remove from the heat and pour the popcorn into a large
bowl. Toss with the salt, black pepper, and Truffle Zest.
Pour the lemon juice into a food-safe spray bottle or
atomizer and spritz the popcorn with it, tossing to evenly
infuse the popcorn with the juice.

SERVES 4

3 SMARTPOINTS PER SERVING

*To really make this recipe
point-friendly, use an air
popper (page 219), which
eliminates the need for any oil.*

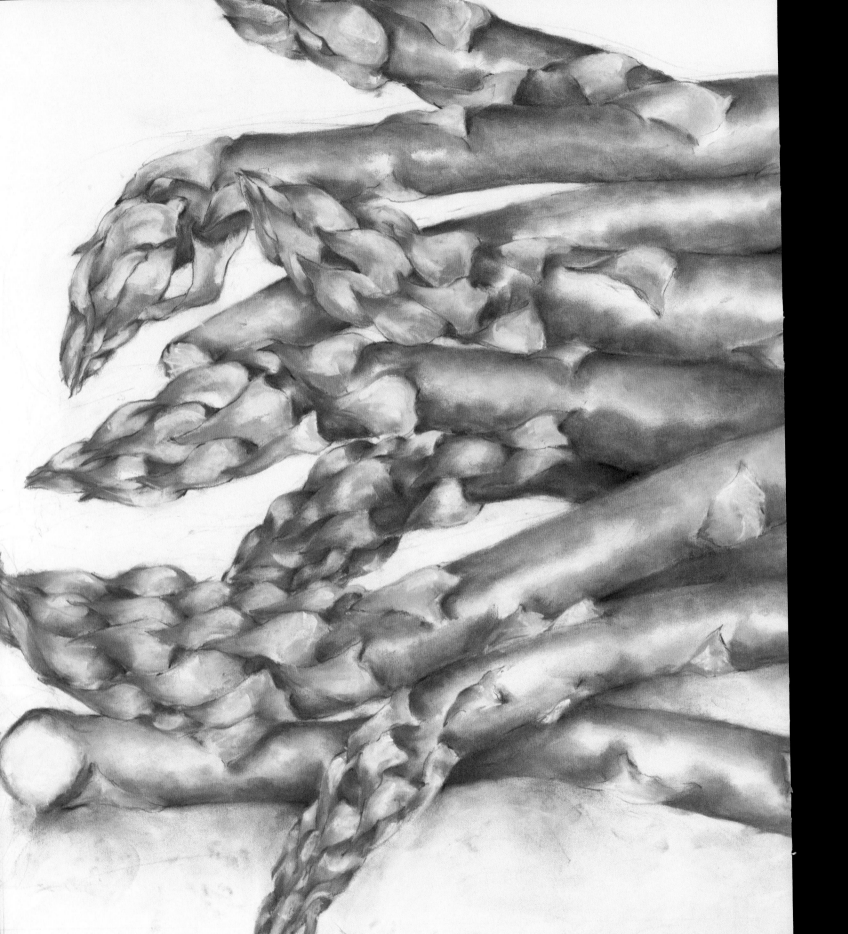

GREENS, GLORIOUS GREENS

THERE I WAS, A LITTLE GIRL, SITTIN' ON THE PORCH SHELLING PEAS AND SHUCKING CORN.

I used to love peeling back the husk and turning those silky blond threads into hair for my homemade doll. The peas were another story. No matter how many peas I pinched—endlessly pinched—from their protective little pods, the bowl never seemed to fill. And how come I had to seed and sow and harvest our vegetables literally from the ground up, while other people—the rich people I always saw on TV—only had to open a can?

I wanted the Jolly Green Giant's peas. But what I really longed for was the feeling I thought buying food from an actual grocery store would give me: the sense that life was lush and plentiful and mine for the taking.

When you know better, you do better.

Yes, there's Maya's refrain again. Sometimes I think she didn't so much pass away from me as she passed into me. Maya, I know a little better now.

And in an effort to do better, there's an edict in my home: We purchase no vegetable that we can grow ourselves. We eat what's in the garden, season by season. As a result, I get my face into the sunshine and my hands into the dirt. The garden work I once disdained, I now embrace. The canned peas I once considered the height of luxury? Not when it's healthier, cheaper, and infinitely more delicious to grow my own. There's much to be said for reaping what you sow. I genuinely appreciate every artichoke when I remember how hard I worked for it. Corn is never sweeter, butter lettuce never softer, and peas—well, I have to admit, I actually delight in shelling them now! The green giants I covet today come straight from the garden, ripe with the vitamins and nutrients our bodies crave. There's Swiss chard, kale, zucchini, collard and turnip greens, of course, and so many varieties of lettuce that you can have a different salad every day of the week. As I do.

I never thought I'd become a "gardenista," but here I am learning about the land with Russell Greenleaf (yes, that's his real name), the farmer at Oprah's Farm on Maui.

Toto, I don't think I'm in Mississippi anymore! But my grandmother would be so proud of these collards!

Nothing's more satisfying than eating what you grow.
If you're a city person try some rosemary on
your fire escape or basil on your window ledge!

OPRAH'S FARM

I used to think of salad as homework, the boring thing you had to get through before you were allowed to play. I had no idea that a gorgeously composed salad—with textures running the gamut from crunchy crispy to impossibly delicate, a rainbow's worth of color, and flavors that register exotic, bitter-sweet, citrusy, nutty, tart, and spicy, sometimes all in the same bite—is by far the most delicious way to play. The key is to dress the salad right (start with a drizzle, give it a good toss, repeat as needed) and feel free to improvise.

Now, when I've got a house filled with ravenous guests, I always make sure—even at breakfast—to have a gorgeous mixed-greens option on the buffet. The salads in this chapter include many of my favorites, the ones I serve again and again. Some are light, some are substantial, all are taste sensations. (And here's a bonus: Just about everything green is zero points!)

I think it's the perfect way to wrap up this food journey we've been on together—with dishes that celebrate nature in all its glory. It may sound corny, but when I eat a good, fresh salad, I can't help thinking of blue skies and warm breezes and how lucky I am to be alive on this beautiful, bountiful earth. So go ahead and help yourself—I've saved the best for last.

HEIRLOOM TOMATO AND SUMMER CORN SALAD WITH TARRAGON VINAIGRETTE

This is like a trip to the farmer's market on a platter! But don't even think about making this in the winter. If the ingredients aren't at peak freshness, it's just not going to work. This salad is also a beautiful base for a simple fillet of grilled fish.

INGREDIENTS:

Vinaigrette

¼ cup rice vinegar

Zest and juice of 1 lemon

½ shallot, chopped

2 teaspoons Dijon-style mustard

1 tablespoon honey

Sea salt

Freshly cracked black pepper

½ cup fresh tarragon leaves

1 cup grapeseed oil

Salad

6 slices prosciutto

4 ears of corn

¼ cup chopped fresh chives

Salt and freshly cracked black pepper

6 medium heirloom tomatoes in a variety of colors

1 medium red onion, thinly sliced into half-moons

6 ounces soft goat cheese

DIRECTIONS:

Preheat the oven to 350°F and line a baking sheet with parchment paper.

To make the vinaigrette: In a blender, combine the vinegar, lemon zest and juice, shallot, mustard, honey, ¾ teaspoon salt, and a few grinds of the pepper mill (page 219) and blend to combine. Add the tarragon, then pour the oil through the hole in the blender lid and blend until emulsified.

To make the salad: Lay the prosciutto out on a baking sheet and bake for 10 to 15 minutes, until mostly crisp. Remove from the oven, cool, and break into bite-size pieces.

Strip the corn of its husks and silk and slice the kernels off. In a medium bowl, combine the corn, chives, and ¼ cup of the vinaigrette. Taste and season with salt and pepper if needed. Cut the tomatoes into thick wedges, place them on a platter, and sprinkle with a bit of salt. Scatter the onion slices around the tomatoes, then spoon the corn and its dressing over the top. Top with the prosciutto, then crumble the goat cheese over everything. Finish with a few grinds of the pepper mill.

The vinaigrette keeps in the refrigerator for up to a week—but something tells me it'll get used up in a couple of days!

PREP TIME	COOK TIME	SERVES	SMARTPOINTS	CALORIES
20 MINUTES	**15** MINUTES	**8**	**6** PER SERVING	**192** PER SERVING

BRUSSELS SPROUT SALAD WITH SHAVED PARMESAN AND MEYER LEMON AND TRUFFLE VINAIGRETTE

You show me someone who doesn't like Brussels sprouts and I'll show you somebody who needs to try this salad! Who knew how good they are when you shred them up and serve them raw with a lemony dressing?

INGREDIENTS:

Zest and juice of 2 Meyer lemons

1 clove garlic, grated on a Microplane

1 teaspoon finely chopped fresh thyme

½ teaspoon Sabatino Truffle Zest

1 teaspoon Sabatino truffle salt

½ teaspoon agave nectar

1 teaspoon truffle oil

4 teaspoons smoked olive oil, such as Castillo de Canena

4 cups shredded Brussels sprouts

¼ teaspoon sea salt

¼ teaspoon freshly ground black pepper

2 cups baby arugula

1 cup fresh flat-leaf parsley leaves

1 ounce great-quality Parmesan cheese, grated on a Microplane

2 tablespoons pine nuts, toasted

DIRECTIONS:

In a small bowl, combine the lemon zest and juice, garlic, thyme, Truffle Zest, truffle salt, agave, truffle oil, and smoked olive oil. Set dressing aside.

Place the Brussels sprouts in a salad bowl. Toss with the sea salt and black pepper. Pour the dressing over the Brussels sprouts, toss well, and set aside for 8 to 10 minutes. Add the baby arugula, parsley, and Parmesan. Divide among serving bowls and top each with toasted pine nuts.

PREP TIME	COOK TIME	SERVES	SMARTPOINTS	CALORIES
15 MINUTES	10 MINUTES	4	4 PER SERVING	168 PER SERVING

Tart and earthy, this salad was a real revelation for me. And it holds its own next to any roast or fish dish.

LENTIL SALAD WITH SPINACH, GOAT CHEESE, POMEGRANATE SEEDS, AND RED ONION GASTRIQUE

I've seen the word "gastrique" on menus, and I've made gastriques at home, but it took Google to tell me what it technically is! Turns out a gastrique is basically a sweet and sour sauce that can be infused with just about anything you want—in this case, red onion. So fancy, yet so simple!

INGREDIENTS:

6 cups water

Salt

1 ½ cups dry beluga or Puy lentils

1 tablespoon extra virgin olive oil

2 medium red onions, thinly sliced into half-moons

1 teaspoon curry powder

¼ cup raisins

1 tablespoon pomegranate molasses

Juice of 2 lemons

Zest and juice of ½ orange

1 teaspoon red pepper flakes

2 cloves garlic, grated on a Microplane

1 teaspoon agave nectar

1 Granny Smith apple, cored and cut into small dice

Freshly ground black pepper

3 cups spinach leaves

¼ cup soft goat cheese, at room temperature

½ cup roasted pumpkin seeds

1 cup pomegranate seeds

DIRECTIONS:

In a medium saucepan, bring 6 cups of water to a boil. Add 2 teaspoons salt and the lentils, return to a boil, then reduce the heat to medium-low and simmer for 25 minutes, or until tender. Drain the lentils and set aside.

Heat the oil in a large sauté pan over medium-high heat. Add the onions and ½ teaspoon salt and cook, stirring occasionally, for 8 to 10 minutes, until lightly browned. Add the curry powder and raisins and cook, stirring, for 5 minutes more. Add the pomegranate molasses and remove from the heat.

Meanwhile, in a medium bowl, whisk together the lemon juice and orange zest and juice, the red pepper flakes, garlic, agave, and 1 teaspoon salt. Add the apple and stir to combine. Season with black pepper.

In a large salad bowl, combine the lentils, red onion mixture, spinach, and apple and let sit for 10 minutes. Crumble in the goat cheese, add the pumpkin seeds and pomegranate seeds, and toss lightly to combine. Divide into bowls and serve.

The juice from pomegranate seeds is said to be three times higher in antioxidant activity than green tea.

PREP TIME	COOK TIME	SERVES	SmartPoints	CALORIES
10 MINUTES	40 MINUTES	8	8 PER SERVING	319 PER SERVING

ROASTED EGGPLANT WITH KALE, FRESH MOZZARELLA, AND PINE NUTS

Given that this dish is only three points, it's an awfully hearty salad with a lot of big flavors.
Serve it with a bowl of soup, and lunch is ready to go!

INGREDIENTS:

6 baby eggplants (about 6 inches long)

Extra virgin olive oil cooking spray

Sea salt

½ bunch Tuscan kale

1 tablespoon extra virgin olive oil

1 clove garlic, grated on a Microplane

2 ounces fresh mozzarella cheese, cut into small cubes

¼ cup currants

½ cup chopped fresh basil

¼ cup fresh flat-leaf parsley leaves

½ cup sliced fresh chives

2 teaspoons balsamic cream

Freshly cracked black pepper

2 tablespoons pine nuts, toasted

DIRECTIONS:

Preheat the oven to 425°F. Slice the eggplant in half lengthwise and place cut side up on a baking sheet. Spritz with cooking spray, sprinkle with salt, and roast for 20 minutes, or until lightly browned.

Meanwhile, remove the stems from the kale, stack the leaves, and thinly slice them. Sprinkle the leaves with ¼ teaspoon salt and rub it in with your hands. Let sit for 10 minutes so the leaves can start to soften.

In a small bowl, combine the oil and garlic. Add to the kale and mix well to coat the leaves in the garlic oil. Fold in the cheese, currants, basil, parsley, and chives. Place the eggplant on a plate and drizzle with the balsamic cream and a little salt and pepper. Top with the kale salad, sprinkle on the pine nuts, and serve.

PREP TIME	COOK TIME	SERVES	SmartPoints	CALORIES
15 MINUTES	20 MINUTES	6	3 PER SERVING	126 PER SERVING

Tuscan kale is also known as "black kale" and "lacinto kale." It's a very crisp, dark, gorgeous green.

TUSCAN KALE AND APPLE SALAD

Perhaps you've begun detecting some common ground among these salad recipes.
Most of them do have an element of sweetness to them. Whether it's honey, agave, apples,
currants, pomegranate seeds, or dried apricots or cranberries, that tiny taste of sweet
always shows up as an interesting wild card against the savory.

INGREDIENTS:

2 tablespoons fresh lemon juice

1 tablespoon apple cider vinegar

¼ teaspoon salt, plus more to taste

¼ teaspoon freshly ground black pepper,
plus more to taste

2 tablespoons extra virgin olive oil

¼ cup dried cranberries

1 bunch Tuscan kale, stemmed and torn into
bite-size pieces

1 head butter lettuce, torn into bite-size pieces

½ bulb fennel, cored and shaved on a mandoline

2 ribs celery, sliced

1 small Gala apple, cored and sliced

1 small Granny Smith apple, cored and sliced

¼ cup walnuts, toasted

DIRECTIONS:

In a small bowl, whisk together the lemon juice,
vinegar, salt, and pepper. Whisk in the oil until
emulsified, then add the dried cranberries. Set aside.

Place the kale in a large bowl, drizzle with 1 tablespoon
of the dressing, and gently massage the leaves for about
a minute to soften them. Add the lettuce, fennel, celery,
and apples. Add the remaining dressing along with the
cranberries. Top with the toasted walnuts and season
with salt and pepper. Spoon into bowls and serve.

PREP TIME	COOK TIME	SERVES	SMARTPOINTS	CALORIES
15 MINUTES	NONE	4	5 PER SERVING	201 PER SERVING

Thanks to the apples and cranberries, this could be a gateway salad for picky eaters!

The reason for using fine sea salt is that the lemon juice is able to dissolve it easily.

GARDEN GREENS WITH LEMON VINAIGRETTE

Fennel, especially when sliced paper thin on the mandoline, adds a very nice twist to even the simplest salad. It's also a wonderful side vegetable when you drizzle the bulb with oil, season with salt and pepper, and roast it.

INGREDIENTS:

Lemon Vinaigrette

1 tablespoon fresh lemon juice

1 clove garlic, grated on a Microplane

¼ teaspoon fine sea salt

¼ teaspoon freshly ground black pepper

1 tablespoon extra virgin olive oil

Salad

2 quarts garden lettuces, cut into bite-size pieces

½ fennel bulb, shaved on a mandoline or sliced very thin so it's translucent

1 cup cherry tomatoes, cut in half

½ cup fresh parsley leaves

1 cup carrots peeled on a julienne peeler

1 cup thinly sliced (on the diagonal) celery

DIRECTIONS:

For the salad: In a salad bowl, combine all ingredients. Add the vinaigrette and toss to coat.

For the vinaigrette: In a small bowl, whisk the lemon juice with the garlic, salt, and pepper. Whisk in the oil until emulsified.

Note: This vinaigrette is very versatile and we use it often as a base that relies on the garden to determine the salad of the day. Some examples are:

Lettuce varieties: mâche, baby gem, romaine, arugula, deer's tongue, frisée, endive, red endive, mizuna, baby beet leaves, watercress

Herbs: flat-leaf parsley, curly parsley, chives, chive blossoms, borage blossoms, cilantro, cilantro blossoms, chervil, mint, basil, purple basil, Thai basil

Vegetables: tomatoes, cherry tomatoes, heirloom tomatoes, bell peppers, jalapeño chiles, celery, jicama, carrots, beets, fennel, corn, peas, green beans

Fruits: Granny Smith apples, Gala apples, peaches, apricots, raisins, dates, oranges, tangerines, Meyer lemons, limes

Nuts: walnuts, hazelnuts, pecans, pistachios, almonds, Marcona almonds, pine nuts

PREP TIME	COOK TIME	SERVES	SmartPoints	CALORIES
10 MINUTES	**NONE**	**4**	**1** PER SERVING	**79** PER SERVING

BUTTER LETTUCE SALAD WITH SMOKY BLUE CHEESE VINAIGRETTE

Here's a salad that manages to supply a creamy blue cheese quality for just two points per serving. It's just further proof that decadence doesn't always have to mean major calories.

INGREDIENTS:

Smoky Blue Cheese Vinaigrette

¼ cup white wine vinegar

2 tablespoons fresh lemon juice

1 tablespoon finely chopped shallots

1 clove garlic, grated on a Microplane

1 teaspoon fine sea salt

½ teaspoon freshly cracked black pepper

2 tablespoons water

¼ cup smoked olive oil, such as Sonoma brand

¼ cup crumbled Rogue Creamery Smokey Blue Cheese or another smoky blue cheese

Salad

2 heads butter lettuce

1 cup cherry tomatoes, cut in half

1 medium ripe Hass avocado, cut in half, pit removed, flesh scooped out and chopped

2 Persian cucumbers, peeled and sliced

1 tablespoon finely diced red onion

Sea salt and freshly ground black pepper

¼ cup fresh parsley leaves

¼ cup small inner fresh basil leaves

DIRECTIONS:

For the vinaigrette: In a small bowl, whisk together the vinegar, lemon juice, shallots, garlic, salt, pepper, and water. Whisk in the oil until emulsified, then add the cheese.

For the salad: Remove the lettuce leaves and wash them in cold water. Dry them in a salad spinner to remove excess water. Tear the lettuce leaves into 2-inch pieces. Lay the leaves on a kitchen towel and refrigerate until ready to use. Place the cherry tomatoes in a salad bowl and add the avocado, cucumbers, and red onion. Mix with 1 tablespoon of the dressing and set aside to marinate for 10 to 30 minutes.

Remove the lettuce leaves from the refrigerator. Toss the leaves in 2 tablespoons dressing. Taste a leaf to be sure it is fully seasoned; add salt and/or pepper if needed. Divide the leaves among 6 plates and top with the cherry tomato mixture and more dressing if needed. Top with the parsley and basil.

PREP TIME	COOK TIME	SERVES	SmartPoints	CALORIES
15 MINUTES	NONE	6	2 PER SERVING	78 PER SERVING

Because it's so delicate and soft, butter lettuce is my very favorite lettuce. Yep, some people like chocolate ice cream better than vanilla; I've actually got a favorite lettuce!

This is a wonderful way to start a meal or a lovely, light entrée lunch salad when grilled shrimp is added.

ROMAINE HEARTS WITH WARM MUSHROOMS AND TRUFFLE VINAIGRETTE

Who says salad has to be cold? Grilling the romaine hearts adds a lovely smoky flavor
that pairs perfectly with the vinaigrette.

INGREDIENTS:

Truffle Vinaigrette

Zest and juice of 2 lemons

2 teaspoons Dijon-style mustard

2 cloves garlic, grated on a Microplane

2 tablespoons Sabatino white truffle oil

2 teaspoons Sabatino Truffle Zest

1 teaspoon Sabatino truffle salt

½ cup extra virgin olive oil

Salad

1 tablespoon grapeseed oil

1 pound cremini or button mushrooms,
stems removed and sliced

1 sprig fresh rosemary

1 teaspoon sea salt

1 shallot, thinly sliced

¼ cup chopped fresh flat-leaf parsley

2 tablespoons thinly sliced fresh chives

3 hearts of romaine lettuce

¼ cup shaved Pecorino Romano cheese

Freshly cracked black pepper

2 tablespoons pine nuts, toasted

DIRECTIONS:

For the vinaigrette: In a medium bowl, whisk
together the lemon zest and juice, the mustard,
grated garlic, truffle oil, Truffle Zest, and truffle
salt. Slowly whisk in the olive oil until the
dressing is emulsified.

For the salad: Heat the oil in a large skillet
over medium-high heat. Add the mushrooms,
rosemary, and salt. Cook until the mushrooms
are starting to soften, about 5 minutes, then add
the shallot and cook, stirring often, until the
mushrooms have caramelized and turned a bit
crispy, about another 10 minutes. The mushrooms
will release some moisture, then will reabsorb it
and begin to brown and crisp. Remove from the
heat, remove the rosemary sprig, and stir in the
parsley and chives.

Cut off the root end of the romaine hearts, slice
them in half lengthwise, and place on individual
plates, cut side up. Spoon the mushrooms over the
hearts, drizzle 1 tablespoon vinaigrette over each,
and sprinkle with the cheese, a little black pepper,
and the pine nuts.

PREP TIME	COOK TIME	SERVES	SmartPoints	CALORIES
10 MINUTES	15 MINUTES	6	5 PER SERVING	196 PER SERVING

TOMATO AND CUCUMBER SALAD

This cool-as-a-cucumber salad is great anytime, but it's particularly
refreshing paired with the spiciness of Indian food.

INGREDIENTS:

3 medium English cucumbers, peeled, seeded,
and chopped

1 pint grape tomatoes, cut in half

¼ medium red onion, finely chopped

¼ cup nonfat plain Greek yogurt

1 tablespoon extra virgin olive oil

Zest and juice of 1 lime

1 teaspoon ground coriander

1 teaspoon sea salt

1 teaspoon freshly ground black pepper

3 tablespoons julienned fresh mint leaves

3 tablespoons julienned fresh basil leaves

DIRECTIONS:

In a salad bowl, combine the cucumber, tomatoes,
and onion. In a small bowl, whisk together the
yogurt, oil, lime zest and juice, coriander, salt, and
pepper. Add to the vegetables and toss to coat.
Add the mint and basil, toss again, and serve.

PREP TIME	COOK TIME	SERVES	SmartPoints	CALORIES
15	NONE	6	1	70
MINUTES			PER SERVING	PER SERVING

*This dish goes great paired with the
Indian Pumpkin Curry on page 119.*

ARTICHOKE SALAD WITH LEMON GARLIC DRESSING

This salad came from my never-ending quest to find ways to use up all the artichokes we grow. They really are one sexy vegetable, maybe because you just have to pull away leaf after leaf before getting to the heart of the matter. But there's also something to be said for a salad that skips the tough stuff and goes straight to something tender.

INGREDIENTS:

Artichokes and marinade

4 large globe artichokes

1 cup white wine

1 tablespoon lemon-flavored extra virgin olive oil, such as Lucini brand

2 cloves garlic, peeled and smashed

2 bay leaves

1 teaspoon salt

Dressing

Juice of 1 lemon

1 clove garlic, minced

¼ teaspoon fine sea salt

¼ teaspoon cracked black pepper

1 tablespoon lemon-flavored extra virgin olive oil, such as Lucini brand

Salad

2 cups baby arugula

2 cups baby field greens

¼ cup fresh-picked cilantro leaves

12 small basil leaves

1 tablespoon Parmesan shavings (shaved with a peeler)

Handful of mustard microgreens

DIRECTIONS:

Prepare the artichokes by cutting the artichoke hearts and bottoms in half and then slicing them ¼ inch thick.

In a medium saucepan, combine the wine, oil, smashed garlic, bay leaves, and salt, place over medium-high heat, and bring to a boil. Add the artichokes, return to a simmer, then reduce the heat, cover, and cook for 2 to 5 minutes, until they are tender. Remove the garlic from the liquid, cool to room temperature, then cover and place the artichokes with their liquid in the refrigerator for about 1 hour to chill.

While the artichokes are chilling, make the dressing: In a small bowl, whisk together the lemon juice, garlic, salt, and pepper. Add the oil and whisk until emulsified.

To assemble the salad: Remove the artichokes from their cooking liquid to a salad bowl and discard the cooking liquid. Add the arugula, field greens, cilantro, and basil, toss, then add the dressing and toss to coat. Spoon into bowls and serve, garnished with the Parmesan and microgreens.

PREP TIME	COOK TIME	SERVES	SMARTPOINTS	CALORIES
20 MINUTES (PLUS 1 HOUR FOR CHILLING)	20 MINUTES	4	4 PER SERVING	211 PER SERVING

CITRUS-AND-HORSERADISH-GLAZED BEETS AND MÂCHE SALAD

This dish includes a lot of disparate flavors that do something magical when brought together! And be sure to use the high-nutrient beet greens either minced into a salad or steamed as a side dish, just the way you'd use spinach or Swiss chard.

INGREDIENTS:

12 baby beets, scrubbed but not peeled

1 tablespoon coarse sea salt

4 sprigs fresh thyme

1 sprig fresh rosemary

1 teaspoon extra virgin olive oil

Dressing

1 cup orange juice

3 tablespoons apple cider vinegar

2 teaspoons unsalted butter

¼ teaspoon ground cardamom

Salt

1½ tablespoons fresh or good-quality bottled horseradish, or to taste

Salad

2 cups mâche lettuce

1 cup baby greens, torn into bite-size pieces

1 teaspoon lemon-flavored extra virgin olive oil, such as Lucini brand

Salt and freshly ground black pepper

1 tablespoon soft goat cheese, at room temperature

¼ cup shelled pistachio nuts

DIRECTIONS:

Preheat the oven to 375°F. Place the beets in a large bowl and toss with the salt, thyme, rosemary, and oil. Transfer the beets from the bowl to a baking sheet lined with aluminum foil. If the beets are different colors, separate them before cooking. Bring the sides of the aluminum foil up to create a sealed package (or separate into two packages if the beets are different colors). Place the beets in the oven and roast for about 45 minutes, until tender when pierced with a knife down the middle.

Let the beets rest for 10 to 15 minutes while you make the glaze. In a small skillet, combine the orange juice, vinegar, butter, and cardamom. Place over medium-high heat and cook until reduced to a glaze consistency, 10 to 15 minutes. Season with salt.

Remove the beets from the foil, then, one at a time, peel them with the assistance of a paper towel. Cut each beet in half, place in a bowl, and toss to coat with the beet glaze. Stir in the horseradish.

To make the salad: combine the mâche and baby greens in a large bowl. Toss with the oil and season with salt and pepper. Crumble in the goat cheese and top with the pistachios. Top the salad with the beets.

PREP TIME	COOK TIME	SERVES	SmartPoints	CALORIES
20 MINUTES	45 MINUTES	4	5 PER SERVING	240 PER SERVING

WILTED SPINACH WITH PANEER

Paneer is a cheese common to Indian, Afghan, Pakistani, and Bangladeshi cuisines. Because it doesn't need any aging, I have it on good authority that it's really easy to make yourself!

INGREDIENTS:

Extra virgin olive oil cooking spray

1 medium yellow onion, finely chopped

1 jalapeño chile, finely chopped

2 tablespoons minced fresh ginger

2 tablespoons minced fresh garlic

1 teaspoon minced fresh turmeric

½ teaspoon curry powder

1 teaspoon ground coriander

½ teaspoon ground cayenne

2 pounds fresh spinach leaves

4 ounces paneer, cut into ½-inch cubes

1 teaspoon salt, plus more if needed

Zest and juice of 1 lemon

Freshly ground black pepper

¼ cup chopped fresh cilantro

DIRECTIONS:

Heat a very large skillet over medium-high heat. Coat the pan with cooking spray, add the onion and jalapeño, and cook, stirring, for 3 minutes, or until starting to soften. Add the ginger, garlic, and turmeric and cook for about 1 minute, until fragrant, covering the pan or adding a tiny bit of water if the mixture starts to stick to the pan. Add the curry powder, coriander, and cayenne and cook, stirring, for 1 minute. Add about a quarter of the spinach and cook, stirring with tongs, until mostly wilted, then continue adding more spinach a little at a time, stirring until all of the spinach is wilted. Stir in the paneer and salt and cook just to warm the paneer through. Remove from the heat and stir in the lemon zest and juice. Taste and add more salt if needed. Remove from the pan to a serving bowl, sprinkle with a little black pepper and the cilantro, and serve.

PREP TIME	COOK TIME	SERVES	SmartPoints	CALORIES
15 MINUTES	10 MINUTES	4	4 PER SERVING	143 PER SERVING

I always keep a knob of fresh ginger in the house! Make it into a tea, and it becomes one of those old-fashioned soothers for everything from an upset tummy to a head cold.

CHOPPED SALAD

Blanching the harder vegetables until they're just al dente makes them texturally consistent with all the other vegetables in the dish. Without a dip in an ice bath afterwards, the vegetables will continue to cook, despite being removed from the burner.

Red Wine Vinaigrette

¼ cup red wine vinegar

2 tablespoons fresh lemon juice

1 small garlic clove, minced

1 tablespoon Dijon-style mustard

½ teaspoon salt, or to taste

¼ teaspoon freshly ground black pepper, or to taste

½ cup extra virgin olive oil

Salad

Salt

½ cup chopped (½-inch pieces) green beans

1 medium carrot, diced

½ cup fresh corn kernels

¼ cup diced red onion

½ red bell pepper, cored and diced

2 medium ribs celery, diced

1 small tomato, seeded and diced

2 cups chopped (½-inch or so pieces) romaine or baby gem lettuce

1 small ripe avocado, cut in half, pit removed, and flesh diced

2 tablespoons thinly sliced fresh chives

4 teaspoons grated Parmesan cheese

Freshly ground black pepper

For the vinaigrette: In a small bowl, whisk together the vinegar, lemon juice, garlic, mustard, salt, and pepper, then slowly whisk in the oil until emulsified. Taste and add more salt and pepper if needed. Whisk again before adding dressing to the salad.

For the salad: Fill a large bowl with water and ice to make an ice-water bath. Bring a medium saucepan of water to a boil and salt it. Add the green beans and cook for about 2 minutes, until starting to soften. Add the carrot and corn and cook for another 1 to 2 minutes, until all the vegetables are crisp-tender. Drain and immediately transfer the vegetables to the ice-water bath to cool. Drain and pat dry with paper towels.

Transfer the blanched vegetables to a salad bowl. Add the onion, bell pepper, celery, and tomato, toss with ¼ cup of the vinaigrette, and set aside to marinate for about 10 minutes. Add the lettuce, avocado, chives, and Parmesan and season with salt and pepper. Divide into bowls and serve.

You can change up this salad by using any vegetables that are fresh and in season.

PREP TIME	COOK TIME	SERVES	SMARTPOINTS	CALORIES
30 MINUTES	NONE	4	5 PER SERVING	177 PER SERVING

ROASTED GARLIC CAESAR

I usually serve this salad at lunch with a crispy chicken thigh. If you decide not
to add any croutons, the salad is just one point, so I generally steer clear of them.
But the choice, as always, is yours.

INGREDIENTS:

Roasted Garlic Caesar Dressing

1 medium head garlic

Extra virgin olive oil cooking spray

1 tablespoon drained capers

1 clove raw garlic

1 tablespoon fresh lime juice

2 teaspoons anchovy paste

2 teaspoons Dijon-style mustard

2 tablespoons reduced-fat mayonnaise

1 tablespoon grated Parmesan cheese

1/4 teaspoon red pepper flakes

1/4 cup red wine vinegar

Sea salt and freshly cracked black pepper to taste

1/3 cup extra virgin olive oil

Salad

1 head romaine lettuce, cut or torn into pieces

1 inner yellow rib celery

2 tablespoons grated Parmesan cheese

DIRECTIONS:

For the dressing: Preheat the oven to 400°F.
Trim the top 1/4 inch off the garlic bulb. Place the
bulb on a piece of aluminum foil large enough to
cover it. Spray the bulb with cooking spray and
sprinkle a little salt over it. Make a package with
the aluminum foil, sealing the ends around the
bulb. Place the garlic in the oven and roast until
the cloves are golden brown and soft, 35 to 40
minutes. Remove the garlic from the oven, and
when it is cool enough to handle, squeeze the
sides of the garlic to remove the creamy cloves
from the outer skin.

In a blender, combine all the ingredients except
the oil and blend to combine. Slowly stream
in the oil through the hole in the lid until all is
added and the dressing is emulsified.

For the salad: In a salad bowl, combine the
lettuce, celery, and Parmesan. Toss well with 1/4
cup of the dressing and serve.

PREP TIME	COOK TIME	SERVES	SMARTPOINTS	CALORIES
10 MINUTES	35–40 MINUTES	4	1 PER SERVING	88 PER SERVING

*If you feel like adding other
vegetables to this Caesar, sun-dried
tomatoes and shaved fennel are both
good choices.*

CHARLIE BIRD'S FARRO SALAD

RECIPE FROM CHEF RYAN HARDY

Farro cooked in water never quite thrilled me, but when you add the cider vinegar, salt, and bay leaf, it's a whole new ball game! Just be sure the farro is "pearled," because it does affect the cooking time.

INGREDIENTS:

1 cup apple cider

2 cups water

Fine sea salt

1 bay leaf

1 cup pearled farro

2 tablespoons extra virgin olive oil

2 tablespoons fresh lemon juice

½ cup shaved Parmesan cheese (shaved with a vegetable peeler)

½ cup chopped pistachios

2 cups arugula leaves

1 cup torn fresh flat-leaf parsley or basil leaves

1 cup torn fresh mint leaves

¾ cup cherry or grape tomatoes, cut in half

⅓ cup thinly sliced radishes

Maldon or other flaky sea salt

DIRECTIONS:

In a medium saucepan, combine the apple cider with 2 cups water, 1 teaspoon fine sea salt, and the bay leaf. Place over high heat and bring to a simmer. Add the farro, return to a simmer, then reduce the heat to medium and simmer until the farro is tender (it will remain chewy in the center), about 30 minutes. Drain any excess liquid from the pan, transfer the farro to a plate, and set aside to cool.

Place the farro in a salad bowl. Add the oil, lemon juice, and a pinch of fine sea salt and stir to coat. Add the Parmesan and pistachios and mix well. The salad base will keep for up to 4 hours at room temperature or overnight in the refrigerator (bring to room temperature before serving).

Just before serving, fold in the arugula, parsley, mint, tomatoes, and radishes. Finish with a little flaky salt, spoon into bowls, and serve.

PREP TIME	COOK TIME	SERVES	SmartPoints	CALORIES
15 MINUTES	30 MINUTES	6	8 PER SERVING	281 PER SERVING

For a more autumnal version of this salad, try trading the tomatoes for some cooked diced squash, pumpkin, or sweet potato!

CRUNCHY SALAD WITH CURRY LIME VINAIGRETTE

Where do I even begin? If a more delightful way to eat your vegetables exists, I sure haven't run into it yet. This is a kaleidoscope of colors and a sophisticated (yet kid-friendly!) blend of textures.

INGREDIENTS:

Dressing

¼ cup apple cider vinegar

2 teaspoons honey

1 clove garlic, grated on a Microplane

1-inch piece ginger, grated on a Microplane

Zest and juice of 2 limes

1 teaspoon curry powder

1 teaspoon salt

3 tablespoons grapeseed oil

Salad

1 cup finely chopped cauliflower florets

1 cup finely chopped broccoli florets

1 cup thinly sliced sugar snap peas

1 cup shredded Brussels sprouts

½ cup shredded red cabbage

½ cup julienned carrots

6 dried apricots, thinly sliced

¼ cup thinly sliced scallions

1 ½ cups chopped mixed herbs such as basil, chives, cilantro, and mint

¼ cup sunflower seeds

¼ cup chopped Marcona almonds

DIRECTIONS:

For the dressing: In a bowl, whisk together the vinegar, honey, garlic, ginger, lime zest and juice, curry powder, and salt. While whisking, slowly add the oil until emulsified.

For the salad: In a salad bowl, combine the cauliflower, broccoli, sugar snap peas, Brussels sprouts, cabbage, carrots, and apricots. Pour the dressing over the salad, mix well, and set aside to marinate for 10 minutes. Add the scallions, herbs, sunflower seeds, and almonds. Divide among individual bowls and serve.

PREP TIME	COOK TIME	SERVES	SMARTPOINTS	CALORIES
15 MINUTES	NONE	6	5 PER SERVING	181 PER SERVING

Marcona almonds from Spain are shorter, rounder, softer, and sweeter than the California variety (shown here), and though nobody would call them low-calorie, just a little bit gives you a bang for your eating buck!

Since this 7,000-year-old grain is so bland, it takes on the flavor of whatever it's cooked with. Don't be afraid to play around. I sometimes cook it in vegetable or chicken stock. It's also a nice oatmeal substitute if you toast it first and then cook it with cinnamon and apples.

QUINOA SALAD

Because it's so sky-high in nutrients and inexpensive to grow, the U.N. believes that quinoa could be instrumental in eradicating hunger! It's a great source of fiber, it's gluten-free, and it's a complete protein.

INGREDIENTS:

Apple Cider Vinaigrette

1 cup apple juice

1 tablespoon finely diced shallot

1 tablespoon fresh thyme leaves

1 tablespoon Dijon-style mustard

¼ cup apple cider vinegar

¼ cup extra virgin olive oil

¼ cup finely diced Granny Smith apple

1 teaspoon fine sea salt

¼ teaspoon freshly ground black pepper

Salad

1 cup quinoa

Fine sea salt

1 medium carrot, cut into ¼-inch cubes

½ medium yellow onion, finely chopped

½ cup jicama, cut into ¼-inch cubes

½ teaspoon finely chopped fresh rosemary

¼ teaspoon dried sage

2 cups roughly chopped Tuscan kale leaves (from about ½ small bunch)

¼ cup toasted hazelnuts, crushed

¼ cup dried cranberries, roughly chopped

DIRECTIONS:

For the vinaigrette: Pour the apple juice into a small saucepan. Add the shallot and thyme, place over medium-high heat, bring to a boil, and boil until reduced by two-thirds, about 10 minutes. Pour into a bowl and set aside to cool to room temperature. Whisk in the mustard, followed by the vinegar, then slowly whisk in the oil until emulsified. Stir in the apple, salt, and pepper.

For the salad: Preheat the oven to 350°F. Put the quinoa on a baking sheet, place in the oven, and toast, stirring a couple of times, for 10 minutes, or until fragrant and golden in color.

Meanwhile, fill a large bowl with ice and water to make an ice-water bath. Fill a large saucepan with water and bring to a boil over high heat. Salt the water, then add the carrot and onion and blanch for 2 to 3 minutes, until crisp-tender. Remove the vegetables with a slotted spoon and briefly submerge them in the ice-water bath to stop the cooking. Remove from the ice-water bath to a plate and pat dry with paper towels.

Return the water to a boil, add the quinoa, and cook for about 10 minutes, until the quinoa germ just starts to open into a tiny curl. Strain the quinoa through a fine-mesh sieve and briefly rinse under cold water. Drain well. Transfer to a serving bowl, add the blanched vegetables, the jicama, rosemary, and sage, and toss with ¼ cup of the dressing (reserve the rest for another salad). Add the kale and toss to coat well in the dressing. Add the hazelnuts and cranberries, taste, and add more salt and pepper if needed. Spoon into bowls and serve.

PREP TIME	COOK TIME	SERVES	SmartPoints	CALORIES
15 MINUTES	20 MINUTES	6	6 PER SERVING	206 PER SERVING

GRILLED ASPARAGUS WITH MIMOSA DRESSING

This is a delightful dish to serve at Easter as a salad or a side dish—
asparagus always seems to declare that spring has sprung.

INGREDIENTS:

Mimosa Dressing

1 large egg

2 teaspoons anchovy paste

Zest and juice of 1 lemon

½ teaspoon fine sea salt

½ teaspoon freshly ground black pepper

¼ teaspoon red pepper flakes

¼ cup lemon-flavored extra virgin olive oil, such as Lucini brand

1 cup chopped fresh parsley leaves

¼ cup fresh basil leaves, cut into ribbons

3 medium scallions, white and green parts, sliced

1 tablespoon finely diced shallot

1 tablespoon drained capers

Asparagus

2 bunches medium asparagus, woody ends snapped off and discarded

Extra virgin olive oil cooking spray

Salt and freshly ground black pepper

DIRECTIONS:

To make the dressing: Place the egg in a small saucepan and add water to cover. Bring to a rolling boil over high heat, cover, then turn off the heat and leave for 10 minutes. Drain, run under cold water to cool, and peel. Separate the yolk and white. Press the white and then the yolk through a mesh strainer (if you don't have one, crumble the yolk and chop the white) and set aside.

In a medium bowl, whisk together the anchovy paste, lemon zest and juice, salt, pepper, red pepper flakes, and oil. Add the egg, parsley, basil, scallions, shallot, and capers and stir to combine.

To make the asparagus: Bring a gas or wood-fired grill to a medium-high heat, or heat a grill pan over medium-high heat. Coat the asparagus lightly with cooking spray and season with salt and pepper. Place the asparagus on the grill or pan and cook for 10 minutes, turning with tongs occasionally, until the asparagus starts to soften and just begins to char at the ends. Using tongs, transfer to a cooling rack. Divide among plates and serve with the dressing poured over the spears.

Think of the Mimosa dressing as an inexpensive and delicious way to add a hit of protein.

PREP TIME	COOK TIME	SERVES	SMARTPOINTS	CALORIES
15 MINUTES	**10** MINUTES	**6**	**3** PER SERVING	**122** PER SERVING

A GUIDE TO MY
FAVORITE GADGETS

Just Chillin'

Mercifully, I've never had a major sweet tooth—but I still want something cool and soothing on occasion. And for people who do crave dessert, while counting points, a sorbet maker is a must. I put it right up there with the fork and dish towel on my list of kitchen essentials.

The panini press is my number one kitchen gadget, because it changed what a sandwich could be. I make this thing for Stedman that I call The Love Sandwich; it's turkey, pepper jack cheese, avocado, tomato, and a little bit of onion—it's nice. But then, when you panini press it, those layers of flavor blend together and everything gets all warm and oozy and grilly and cheesy and melty. Believe me, love doesn't begin to describe it!

A Pressing Matter

The bad news about the Japanese mandoline is that it's very sharp and if you're not extremely careful with it, you can end up with a finger that looks like it has the lead in a Quentin Tarantino movie. The good news is you can shave vegetables paper thin that a slice of zucchini or asparagus becomes a ribbon of pasta and a potato becomes the perfect chip.

Shear Genius

1/4 TSP / 1.2 ML

Measure for Measure

When you've been at it long enough, you instinctively a feel for the difference between two teaspoons and tablespoon, but unless you're very accurate, using a measuring spoon is a really smart move.

Grate Expectations

Wanna know what half an ounce of Parmesan cheese, which is only two points, looks like when you use a Microplane on it? It looks like a fluffy mountain of cheese! The Microplane grates it so fine and airy that a little goes a long, long, long way! It's especially good for truffles, if you just want a light dusting over your eggs or pasta

These are my go-to gadgets. Meaning I keep them in my kitchen and I use them all week long. But my advice is to really ask yourself if you'll actually work with these tools on a regular basis or if they're more likely to land in the seemed-like-a-good-idea-at-the-time closet. Oh, and one more thought: While I like these particular brands, the products below are available at every price point, so I quote Smokey Robinson when I say, "You better shop around!"

I like this popcorn popper because it has a little area for melted butter right next to it for when we have guests who aren't counting points. But for people who find the whole melted butter thing a little heavy, I put lemon in an atomizer, and I spray it over the air-popped corn. Then I add Truffle Zest and a pinch of truffle salt, because truffles and lemon are the greatest combination since rhythm and blues. If I really want to get decadent, I Microplane an ounce of Parmesan cheese over the whole thing. I promise, you'll never miss the butter.

Screen Gems

Transformers

They say the first taste is with your eyes. Well, the Spiralizer turns beets, carrots, and parsnips into a delicate tangle of color and texture for salads and garnishes, but I mostly use it to convert an ordinary zucchini into a very virtuous bowl of spaghetti. Best of all, you don't need a degree in aerodynamics and three years on the Ford assembly line to put it together or take it apart to clean.

Mount Tellicherry, on India's Malabar Coast, is home to the largest and ripest "Tellicherry" peppercorns, which is what I fill my pepper mill with. I'm crazy for this Atlas mill because the design is ergonomically sympathetic to my wrist, it lets me adjust the texture from coarse to medium to fine, and the hardened steel cutting mechanism grinds rather than smashes the peppercorns, which maximizes flavor and aroma. But be careful; Tellicherries are extremely fragrant—so either proceed with caution or brace for the kind of sneeze seldom seen outside of cartoons.

Let's Play Pepper

The Cutting Edge

An excellent knife can be the difference between cooking and drudgery. It's an investment, but you won't be sorry you made it because if you treat your knife well—don't put it in the dishwasher, do get it sharpened once in a while—you'll have it for the rest of your life.

Scaling Back

When you're trying to change your eating habits, it's essential that you really understand portion control. At first, you'll be amazed what three ounces of fish actually looks like, but before long the scale will be strictly for confirming your well-educated guess.

FINDING A NEW PATH ON MY JOURNEY WITH FOOD

When I decided to write this book a while back, I took a long look at myself in a full-length mirror. From the top of my ponytailed head down to the bunioned feet I inherited from my father, I just stood very still, very naked, staring in the mirror. Pretty soon a quiet little mantra emerged: Thank you. Thank you. Thank you. I began thinking about all the times I've been so critical, so judgmental of this body that has carried me through nearly 63 years. Thank you, I said. Thank you for allowing me, as the old folks used to say in church, to wake up clothed in my right mind. Thank you. Thank you for shoulders that are sturdy and knees that still work. Thank you. Thank you for allowing me to walk and to stand and to make myself fully awake. And thank you for letting me share that hard-earned consciousness.

I'm not looking back, I'm not running ahead. The time is now, the place is here.

Meister Eckhart, a theologian and mystic born in the year 1260, said something so true that it has endured for centuries: "If the only prayer you ever say in your entire life is thank you, it will be enough." I've come to understand that I am blessed to begin each day with enough. That I have enough. That I am enough. The moment I open my eyes, my first thought is always the same: *Thank you*. I then spend anywhere from five to 20 minutes just being with the silence. I take in the stillness that surrounds me. As I said in chapter 4, I pray and I meditate, two activities that, in my mind, are always one and the same; the practice anchors me to the beat of my own heart and gives me a vital sense of order. Next, I'm ready to go out for a walk with my fur family, Luke, Laila, Sadie, Sunny, and Lauren. I don't know if it's the feel of the breeze, the smell of the grass, or the knowledge that there's another frolicking day in their future, but they're totally carefree—one more reason for gratitude. We come back inside and I devote the next 45 minutes or so to exercising up a good sweat. That's my daily ritual.

As for food, I eat breakfast, lunch, and dinner, and allow for two snacks. I track my points. I try my best to remain consciously in the game—mindful of what I'm eating, thinking, and doing. I weigh myself periodically, but I'm focused on life beyond the scale. I've lost over 40 pounds since I started Weight Watchers; maybe it'll be 50 by the time you read this, or maybe it won't. I no longer have a target weight I'm desperate to hit or a destination I'm rushing to reach.

These days my goal is a lot more worthwhile: to end my battle with weight without feeling guilt or shame—without the critic in my head hissing, *You blew it!* I embrace my practice of counting points as a tool to help me reframe my attitude, redirect my thinking, and reform my old habits. I hold myself accountable, but I don't take myself to task. I'm stepping up and out of my own history and into the light of self-awareness, acceptance, and love. I'm moving forward with better health and a happiness so deep and rewarding that I have a new favorite word for it: contentment. I finally get to make peace with my story of food. And I wish the very same for you.

"TO LOVE YOURSELF IS
A NEVER-ENDING PROCESS."

—OPRAH WINFREY

A NOTE ABOUT WEIGHT WATCHERS
SMARTPOINTS

As I mentioned, I treat Weight Watchers SmartPoints almost like a game. Every food is assigned a SmartPoints value—one easy-to-use number based on four components: calories, saturated fat, sugar, and protein. If you decide you want to give it a try, you'll get a personalized SmartPoints Budget based on your height, weight, gender, and age, and you can spend those points on any food you like. With SmartPoints, everything is still on the menu!

For more information about SmartPoints, go to www.weightwatchers.com

MEET THE CHEFS

Eduardo Chavez became a beloved member of the California community where I live by helping to manage everyone's parties. He greeted each guest by name and always remembered what they drank. I stood back and marveled at his gift for putting people instantly at ease. Eddie's gift for naming dishes is another story—everything is sexy this and sexy that. If by sexy he means spicy, earthy, and gorgeous, then he does have a point. Check out his very sexy drinks on page 164.

I've already told you how I met **Rosie Daley** when she cooked for me at the spa I was visiting. What I didn't tell you about was stopping at farm stands and apple orchards with her, watching the extraordinary way she removed the fat but maintained the flavor in every dish she prepared, and how many laughs we shared hanging out in the kitchen! Try her wonderful Peppered Tuna recipe on page 133.

I was introduced to **Taryn Huebner** in Chicago and hired her to cook for me at work. Many times her food and snacks provided just the solace and comfort I needed to get through those long days of tapings and meetings. Taryn's got an incredible gift for putting together unexpected combinations. Try her Turkey Burger recipe on page 160, and you'll see exactly what I mean.

Two Christmases ago I had twenty-four guests for dinner, and **Mei Lin**, who had just won *Top Chef,* came to help out in the kitchen. I took a special liking to the Asian influence Mei brings to her specialties, and I also fell in love with her Turkey Lasagna (page 63)—it's the best I've ever had!

Art Smith has a Southern soul, and it has always spoken directly to me. I could tell you about all the fantastic meals he made over the eight years he cooked for me and Stedman, but his real specialty is bringing people together over an unforgettable meal. Art's Unfried Chicken (page 60) is excellent, but if you decide to splurge, his Fried Chicken (page 59) is beyond spectacular!

Finding **Sonny Sweetman** was pure serendipity. I had taken twelve of my girls from South Africa for an impromptu tea at a hotel I've always loved in Los Angeles. The hostess explained that they only did tea on the weekends. But Sonny popped out of the kitchen and saved the day, whipping up a spread fit for Buckingham Palace! He made everything from finger sandwiches to scones. Stedman calls him "the scientist" because he makes each meal with such detail and precision. Try his amazing Halibut à la Grecque on page 84.

INDEX

CREDITS AND ACKNOWLEDGMENTS

MELCHER MEDIA

President and CEO: Charles Melcher

Vice President and COO: Bonnie Eldon

Senior Editor/Producer: Aaron Kenedi

Production Manager: Susan Lynch

Digital Producer: Shannon Fanuko

Editorial Assistant: Victoria Spencer

Recipe Editor and Developer: Leda Scheintaub

Food Photographer: Tina Rupp

Prop Stylist: Stephanie Hanes

Food Stylist: Carrie Purcell

O MAGAZINE

Art Direction: Adam B. Glassman

Contributing Editorial: Deborah Way

Makeup: Derrick Rutledge

Hair: Nicole Mangrum

Stylist: Jenny Capitain

Flowers in Maui: Diana Dolan,
Porch, Carpinteria, CA

Flowers in Telluride: Kristin Undhjem
of gardenstorehome.com

WEIGHT WATCHERS

Calorie and SmartPoints values provided by
Maria Kinirons, RDN, Weight Watchers

MELCHER MEDIA WOULD LIKE TO THANK:

Callie Barlow, Jess Bass, Trina Bentley, Emma Blackwood, Amelie Cherlin, Karl Daum, Barbara Gogan, Heather Hughes, Luke Jarvis, Maria Kinirons, Kaarina Mackenzie, Karolina Manko, Sarah Melton, John Morgan, Lauren Nathan, Nola Romano, Laura Roumanos, Rachel Schlotfeldt, Suchan Vodoor, Megan Worman, Katy Yudin